pact Analysis
of Poverty Alleviation Programmes
and Projects

SOCIAL IMPACT ANALYSIS OF POVERTY ALLEVIATION PROGRAMMES AND PROJECTS

A Contribution to the Debate on the Methodology of Evaluation in Development Cooperation

SUSANNE NEUBERT

FRANK CASS
LONDON • PORTLAND, OR
Published in association with the
German Development Institute, Berlin

First published in 2000 in Great Britain by
FRANK CASS PUBLISHERS
Newbury House, 900 Eastern Avenue,
London IG2 7HH

and in the United States of America by
FRANK CASS PUBLISHERS
c/o ISBS
5804 N.E. Hassalo Street
Portland, Oregon 97213-3644

Website: www.frankcass.com

Copyright © 2000 GDI/Frank Cass

British Library Cataloguing in Publication Data

Neubert, Susanne
  Social impact analysis of poverty alleviation programmes
  and projects : a contribution to the debate on the
  methodology of evaluation in development cooperation. –
  (GDI book series ; no. 14)
  1. Poverty – Prevention – Research 2. Evaluation research
  (Social action programs)
  I. Title
  362.5'8'072

  ISBN 0-7146-5049-8 (cased)
  ISBN 0-7146-8151-2 (paper)

Library of Congress Cataloging-in-Publication Data

Neubert, Susanne, 1958–
  Social impact analysis of poverty alleviation programmes and projects : a contribution
to the debate on the methodology of evaluation in development cooperation / Susanne Neubert.
    p. cm. – (GDI book series, ISSN 1460-4175 : no. 14)
  Includes bibliographical references.
  ISBN 0-7146-5049-8 (cased). – ISBN 0-7146-8151-2 (paper)
    1. Economic assistance, Domestic–Social aspects. 2. Economic development projects.
  I. Title. II. Series.

HC79.P63 N48 2000
362.5'8–dc21   00-022704

Printed and bound in Great Britain by
Antony Rowe Ltd, Chippenham, Wilts

Preface

The method of impact assessment of poverty alleviation projects (MAPP) elaborated and presented in this study demonstrates a new way of operationalizing social development at programme level and of evaluating the effectiveness of development programmes and projects in the context of the lives of the target groups. The new method was devised during a debate with German development cooperation institutions, such as the Federal German Ministry for Economic Cooperation and Development (BMZ) and donor organizations, and with counterpart organizations and target groups. The emphasis was placed on the development of a standardized and thus replicable procedure for recording the social impact of project and programme operations at an acceptable level of evaluation effort.

This study was carried out at the German Development Institute (GDI) in Berlin. The field research and evaluations of the literature were completed in mid-1998.

I should like to thank everyone who helped me in many different ways as I undertook this study, especially the people of Mali, i.e. the target groups of the *Projet de Gestion des Ressources Naturelles* (PGRN), who analysed the impact of the project with great commitment. My thanks too to Andreas von Ramdohr, Niko von der Lühe, Eckhard Dudeck and Fatim Haidara, colleagues at the German Agency for Technical Cooperation (GTZ), for their generous support during the evaluation process.

The description of evaluation as it is undertaken in Germany is based on a number of interviews. I am very grateful to the staff of the BMZ, KfW, GTZ, DED, KAS, FES, HBS and EZE for the information they have provided and especially to Volker Steigerwald for his help and criticism as the study emerged. Success in the further development of the methodology of social project evaluation will also continue to depend primarily on the institutions and people I have mentioned.

I also wish to thank the professionals of the German Development Institute for their support and for the discussions we have had.

Berlin, November 1999   Susanne Neubert

Contents

Abbreviations

ADB	Asian Development Bank
AEA	Agro-ecosystems Analysis
BA	Beneficiary Assessment
BMZ	Bundesministrium für wirtschaftliche Zusammenarbeit und Entwicklung (Federal Ministry for Economic Cooperation and Development)
CDG	Carl Duisberg-Gesellschaft (Carl Duisberg Society)
CVGRN	Comité Villageois de Gestion des Ressources Naturelles
DAC	Development Assistance Committee
DED	Deutscher Entwicklungsdienst (German Development Service)
DFID	Department for International Development
EZE	Evangelische Zentralstelle für Entwicklungshilfe (Development Aid Centre of the Protestant Church in Germany)
FCFA	Franc de la Communauté Financière Africaine
FES	Friedrich-Ebert-Stiftung (Friedrich Ebert Foundation)
GTZ	Deutsche Gesellschaft für Technische Zusammenarbeit (German Agency for Technical Cooperation)
HBS	Heinrich-Böll-Stiftung (Heinrich Böll Foundation)
HDR	Human Development Report
HWWA	Hamburger Institut für Wirtschaftsforschung (Hamburg Institute for Economic Research; formerly Hamburger Weltwirtschaftliches Archiv)
IDS	Institute of Development Studies
IFAD	International Fund for Agricultural Development
IJA	Initiative pour les Jeunes Aveugles

KAS	Konrad-Adenauer-Stiftung (Konrad Adenauer Foundation)
KfW	Kreditanstalt für Wiederaufbau (the German Development Bank)
M&E	monitoring and evaluation
NGO	Non-governmental Organization
NRAC	Natural Resources Advisers Conference
NRPAD	Natural Resources Policy and Advisory Department
ODA	Overseas Development Administration (now DFID)
OECD	Organization for Economic Co-operation and Development
OED	Operations Evaluation Department
PAR	Participatory Action Research
PE	Participatory Evaluation
PGRN	Projet de Gestion des Ressources Naturelles
PIDEB	Programme Intégré de Développement de Bafoulabé
PPR	Project Progress Review
PRA	Participatory Rural Appraisal
RA	Regional Assistant
RSA	Rapid Social Assessment
SRL	Sustainable Rural Livelihood
TGA	Target-group Analysis
TOR	Terms of Reference
UNDP	United Nations Development Programme
ZOPP	Zielorientierte Programmplanung (Objectives-oriented Project Planning)

Summary

Development organizations are busily searching for concepts and methods that will enable impacts of development cooperation to be recorded and scientifically tenable, transparent and practicable conclusions to be drawn. They rightly expect the cost of evaluations to be proportional to the project budget. While a standardized set of tools is available for the economic and technical evaluation of projects, methods of covering the social dimension, which are of prime importance for impact analysis, have yet to reach maturity. This study considers the state of research on evaluation that includes the social dimension and the methods used. A new method of impact assessment of poverty alleviation projects (MAPP) is also presented and underpinned empirically. MAPP is based on a multidimensional conception of poverty and shows how the social dimension can be operationalized with the aid of four key social processes: *improvement of livelihoods, access to resources, expansion of knowledge* and *participation in rights*. MAPP makes it possible to determine whether the poverty of the target groups has actually been alleviated and, if so, how the benefits of the project have been distributed among the various social groups, e.g. by gender and socio-professional categories.

The social dimension in development cooperation and the concept of poverty

"Social" means *"concerning the order of human society"* and refers to the relationship between individuals, between individuals and groups and between groups within a society. According to a *World Bank* definition, *social dimension* means the **welfare of human beings**, i.e. their quality of life, their education and the quality and sustainability of their institutions and relations. In the development policy context the social dimension is a cross-section criterion that becomes effective in a cultural, political and economic dimension.

Until a few years ago the social dimension was not regarded as an important planning and evaluation level of development cooperation. Although initial steps towards operationalizing socio-economic impacts were developed by the research community as part of the basic needs approach of the 1970s, the social dimension has been the focus of project evaluation only since the public debate on the effectiveness of development projects began and the legitimacy of the whole area of development cooperation policy was questioned.

In a social impact analysis the poverty-reducing effects of a project and their distribution among individuals and social groups are examined. The equation of "poverty reduction or alleviation" with "social development" is based on a multidimensional view of "poverty", as taken by the *United Nations Development Programme* (UNDP).

Various development organizations are endeavouring to operationalize social development. Some years before working groups of the World Bank and the *Department for International Development* (DFID) devised framework concepts for the macro and meso levels, the *Overseas Development Administration* (ODA) (renamed the Department for International Development (DFID) in May 1997) presented a concept for key social processes under which all the relevant social categories can be subsumed and which include the improvement of livelihoods, access to resources, the expansion of knowledge and participation in rights. This division is used in MAPP as the basis for operationalization at micro and meso level and also proves to be compatible with the framework concepts referred to above.

Tendencies in German evaluation

The past two years have seen a lively debate on evaluation methods in German governmental and non-governmental development cooperation, involving the various development organizations and, more recently, the research community. Despite the convergence of views in Germany, the objectives and interests of specific organizations are associated with evaluations. While ex post analyses are gaining in importance for the BMZ – and for evaluations undertaken by the KfW – and the supervisory function of evaluations will continue to play an important role in the future, the GTZ and DED see evaluations primarily as "management tools", used to oversee projects. The BMZ believes that the findings of evaluations should enable decisions to be taken on development policy and strategy relating to a range of programmes and projects, but for organizations engaged in technical and human resources cooperation their main purpose is to ensure institutional and joint learning. The involvement of the partner and target groups is taken as a matter of course in this context. This view conforms to the GTZ's client-oriented quality concept for the evaluation of "technical cooperation services" and the DED's conception of partnership. According to their various objectives, the BMZ's and KfW's evaluations are conducted primarily by external experts, whereas the GTZ clearly prefers self-evaluation.

For the **Church organizations** cooperation is based on the idea of solidarity and their partners' autonomy, and the partners consequently bear full responsibility for all phases of projects, including evaluation. They believe that the donor's activity in evaluations should focus on the improvement of the partner's evaluation capacities, should this be necessary. Church organizations are, however, sceptical of the efforts of governmental organizations to increase efficiency which impact analyses reveal, since solidarity based on Christian motives may in certain cases extend beyond the principle of aid being used as effectively as possible. Nonetheless, this conviction should not, as a matter of principle, prevent Church organizations from carrying out evaluations on the basis of efficiency criteria.

The causality problem and evaluation designs

All development organizations refer to the need for practicable and cheap methods of carrying out impact analyses. The most serious methodological problem in this context lies in being certain that impacts are ascribed to the right project operations. From the strictly scientific angle evidence of a link between cause and effect can be found only with the help of an **experimental evaluation design** in which a test group, which has been exposed to project measures, is compared to a control group, which has not been exposed to project measures (**with-and-without comparison**). Only then can "external interference factors" be isolated and "net effects" clearly identified. A design of this nature presupposes the qualitative comparability of test and control groups, since it is assumed that like measures have like effects. This is in fact very difficult to achieve, and the creation of control groups therefore poses major problems. An argument against the experimental approach, moreover, is that these procedures neglect actual conditions. They are expensive and time-consuming, and the control group, which is seen as the "zero variant", is deemed to be entirely passive. This view is inconsistent with the idea of partnership and the goal of participation that is inalienably linked to the present conception of development cooperation.

An alternative to the with-and-without comparison is the **before-and-after comparison**, in which the test group forms its own control group. A design of this nature implies that the environment remains the same during the project cycle and that the impacts identified are not adversely affected by the influence of other processes. As this is unrealistic, it produces valid findings only if the number of "test groups" examined is sufficiently large for the interference factors to be eliminated by means of statistical procedures. In practice, before-and-after comparisons often fail because the results of a prior examination are not available when the impact evaluation contract is awarded. Consequently, evaluations made with the aid of "shadow checks", a grey area of scientific analysis, dominate in practice. They are based on experts' personal and collective judgements, i.e. their experience and the secondary information available to them are used to estimate what would have happened if the measures had not been taken.

Owing to the methodological difficulties posed by scientifically rigorous and quantitatively oriented evaluation designs the tendency today is to abandon the causality goal in favour of increased plausibility. Attempts should, however, be made to raise the level of plausibility through the introduction of new methodological elements and so to narrow the attribution gap.

Practical evaluations these days normally proceed from the angle of the project, the outputs being evaluated on the basis of the project inputs and data on the outcomes rarely existing. Even when outcome data are included in the evaluation, the range of this approach, being closely geared to the project, is too limited for impacts to be recorded and for unintentional impacts to be recognized. One way of increasing the range and including unintentional impacts is to add context-related data (results on the ground) that shed light on the changing lives of the people. Contrasting project- and context-related data also enables further conclusions to be drawn on the "social efficiency" of project inputs.

In both project-related and context-related evaluation the question of inquiry methods arises. In recent years the participatory approach has become increasingly popular with development organizations. In **participatory evaluation** the intention is to close the social and cognitive gap between domestic and foreign project staff and the target groups. Although the scientific research community is sceptical about the participatory approach, claiming that subjective data are of limited validity, the approach advocated here is based on **constructivism** and on a concept of validity that has been modified accordingly. All opinions, according to this view, contribute to the identification of reality, even though each describes only one facet of reality. Subjectivity is not seen as an obstacle to establishing the truth: the inclusion of all assessments is most likely to lead to a form of reality that is valid for everyone.

Indicators are commonly used to record complex phenomena in evaluation. The problem of forming and weighting indicators is not discussed exhaustively in this study. It is considered only in the context of MAPP. Accordingly, the social situation in a region or community cannot, for example, be described by reference to a single indicator: several need to be consulted. Proceeding from this angle, the key social processes are taken as basic indicators in accordance with the ODA's concept. It is also assumed that the significance of the various social criteria is not constant, but that they change in importance for the quality of life from one time and place to another. The principle that applies in this context is that only if all key social processes are within the optimum range can the full human potential be achieved. This analogy with the law of limiting factors also means that below a certain threshold any key factor is capable of preventing social development.

From conventional to participatory inquiry methods

The **inquiry methods** used in evaluation are based partly on the study of secondary sources, but mainly on semi-structured interviews of key informants. Besides providing descriptive information, interviews make for an understanding of motivations and values and are suitable for the creative development of proposals for solving problems. If, however, the idea of **participatory evaluation** is adopted, a participatory approach must also be adopted during the collection of data. The past ten years have seen the development of numerous participatory inquiry methods, the best known in development cooperation being *participatory rural appraisal* (PRA). PRA is based on certain key concepts, the most important elements of which are "triangulation", "communal learning" and "optimal ignorance". Triangulation is a form of cross-checking the composition of the team, the sources of information and the techniques used. Communal learning concerns an improved understanding of the mutual perceptions of reality of domestic and foreign project staff and the target group through the joint achievement of evaluation results. The aim of optimal ignorance, on the other hand, is to avoid unnecessary accuracy during the collection of data and to direct attention sustainably to what is essential. In principle, the PRA methodology very often operates with visualizations, both quantitative and qualitative appraisals being undertaken. In practice, however, qualitative methods are preferred. The main risk with the PRA approach is that it may lead to excessive differentiation, i.e. high specificity of results and limited result orientation. This may adversely affect the comparability of investigations, and endless communication loops may turn the originally rapid and goal-oriented approach into an expensive and inefficient procedure.

MAPP, a new method of impact assessment of poverty alleviation projects

MAPP is based on the application of PRA inquiry techniques modified to enable them to be used for impact evaluations and combined to form a logically structured and result-oriented system. The context-related evaluation design consists of hypothetical "before-and-after comparisons" of the changing lives of the people in the project region, the data required being collected with the aid of the systematized memories of the target groups. For cross-checking purposes information is also obtained through direct observation and the project's M&E system. The main evaluation tool is the open group discussion, in which all social sub-groups should as far as possible be represented. If this does not give rise to a genuine discourse, separate group meetings can be held.

The five MAPP instruments that build on each other and the ensuing quantification stage are explained in the following:

(1) "Life line" $\Rightarrow$ identifying the minimum factors of life

On the basis of a five-point system the target groups establish a life line which shows the annual change in their perception of their quality of life in recent decades. The deciding factor for a given score may vary every year and is interpreted as the case-by-case minimum factor over a given period.

(2) "Trend analysis" $\Rightarrow$ painting a differentiated picture of social development in the village

With the help of a "social trend analysis" a profile of the social community is drawn in each case, showing – again on a five-point scale – how it has changed in recent years. The trend analysis reveals the "gross effects" within the project cycle for all social criteria. The various causes of changes are described.

(3) "Activity list" $\Rightarrow$ determining the importance of and effort expended on project activities, identifying the beneficiary sub-groups

All project activities and project sponsors are entered in a table. The importance of each activity for the everyday life of the target groups is evaluated, and the beneficiary groups are identified. Points are then awarded for the effort involved in implementing and maintaining the measures. The activity list provides the data for estimating the cost-benefit ratio of project activities at the level of the social community and enables the contributions made by the various donor organizations to be differentiated.

(4)   "Influence matrix" $\Rightarrow$ attribution of impacts to project activities

The strength of the impact of each project activity on the social criteria is evaluated, again on a five-point scale. Active and passive totals are formed, revealing the most influenced social criterion on one axis and the most influential project activity on the other. The influence matrix sheds light on the perceived "net influences" of the project measures.

(5)   "Transects" $\Rightarrow$ cross-section of the community

All visible project measures in the community are inspected by the evaluation team, and the team's external perception is compared to the target groups' own perception. This enables the information provided by the target groups to be better understood and classified.

(6)   Establishment of the development and impact profile

On the basis of the data collected a "development and impact profile" is now established to indicate the development of each criterion within the project cycle on a scale of five. The various causes of trends and fluctuations are indicated, and the factors that have given rise to them are identified.

Results of the test run in a resource management programme

MAPP was tested in a resource management programme (PGRN) in Mali that is being assisted by the World Bank and GTZ ("*Projet de gestion des Ressources Naturelles*/PGRN" of the Ministry of Rural Development and the Environment in Bamako). Three villages in the Bafoulabé region, one of which had only recently begun to cooperate, the other two having worked with the project for the past seven years, were chosen as examples. In principle, the aim of the project is to enable the people to use the land sustainably on the basis of land use plans in whose establishment they participate and so to halt the process of degradation and to reduce poverty. The test run was made jointly by a three-person evaluation team and the target groups and produced the following results:

The **life lines** show that the influence of the PGRN needs to be assessed against the background of the quantity of rainfall, which is regarded as a minimum factor of the region. The quantity and distribution of rainfall determine the agricultural yields, which are in turn the main determinant of survival prospects and the perceived quality of life in the region. Although the PGRN cannot compensate for serious droughts or prevent the resulting migration, its influence is visible where fluctuations in rainfall lead to less pronounced changes in the quality of life.

The **trend analyses** reveal positive social developments in all three villages. In the two villages that have been involved in the project for some years a very positive trend in, respectively, eight and four of the social criteria is to be seen within the project cycle. In particular, access to resources, knowledge of sustainable land use and the proportion of children enrolled in education rose significantly. However, the criteria that describe living standards did not develop in any clear direction. The health status of the children in two villages tended to worsen. This was due to several measles and meningitis epidemics in recent years, which were not treated early enough despite the existence of a health station. In two villages the conflict between farmers and herders also worsened. Directly linked to the PGRN were land use conflicts due to the establishment of nature reserves, tree plantations and anti-erosion stone lines and to newly defined paths to be taken by the herds to reach the grazing areas. For various reasons – that will be mentioned in chapter 5 – the herders tend not to respect the agreements on land use and to allow their herds to wander about and destroy some of the facilities.

The **activity lists** reveal that in all the villages a wide range of operations is being assisted by various organizations. Most measures in the villages are, however, due to support from the PGRN. In all the villages the community projects, i.e. the school, health station and grain bank, are obviously of outstanding importance for the people. The "productive operations" benefit only some of the people, primarily men engaged in arable farming. What the people usually invest in the activities is their labour. The work is distributed "fairly", i.e. it is performed by those who also derive benefit from the measure.

The **active sides** of the **influence matrices** show that equipping the people with donkey carts is the key activity of the project. Increased mobility helps both to improve living standards and to facilitate access to resources. As regards the availability of firewood, however, the carts are of questionable benefit, since the growing shortage of wood will merely be concealed for a brief period, not minimized, by the increase in the radius over which it can be collected. Moreover, increased mobility usually benefits the men, since the women do not as a rule have donkey carts and are not used to acquiring them. In some villages this is offset by the fact that the men lend their wives the carts to go to market, for example. The subsidization of the carts is linked to resource protection measures, which only the men are able to decide to implement owing to land use rights.

On the **passive side** the matrices show that "knowledge of sustainable land use" in particular is being improved by the project activities. However, the activities also have a positive influence on the living standard criteria in many ways. The fact that the impacts on living standards are visible only in the influence matrices and not in the trend analyses is due to the external factors that overshadow and continue to cancel out the positive effectiveness of the project operations in the trend analyses virtually as interference factors.

The **development and impact profiles** show that the positive social developments in the villages that have participated in the project for some years are due not only to the commitment of the people but also to the PGRN, whereas the impacts in the village that began to cooperate comparatively recently are less pronounced or can be partly ascribed to the work of another organization. Although the development of living standards does not yet depend directly on the PGRN, a positive trend that can be attributed to the grain bank financed by the PGRN is to be seen in family incomes in the villages that have participated in the project for some time. The PGRN has had its main impact in "accessibility of resources", and the subsidization of the donkey carts plays a key role in this context, as already mentioned. The increase in the knowledge of sustainable land use is also directly attributable to the PGRN, while the very sharp rise in the number of children attending school can be ascribed to the people's own commitment and the work of other organizations and government services.

Three factors, however, pose a threat to positive social development in the villages: the deteriorating health status of the children, the growing shortage of firewood and the worsening conflict between farmers and herders and, in some villages, between men and women. The negative trend in the first factor stems from organizational shortcomings in the health sector, in which the PGRN is not involved and for which it is therefore no more than indirectly responsible. As regards the access to firewood, the use of the donkey carts is a two-edged sword: Although its use in the search for firewood is offsetting the shortage in two villages in the short term, the increased radius over which wood can be collected is simply hastening the desertification process in the longer term. It takes a long time before the trees planted can be used for firewood and the plantations are too small. The growing land use conflicts between the socio-professional groups are primarily due to external factors. Because of its work in the resource sphere, however, the project gives rise to areas of friction in which old conflicts are re-emerging. The PGRN has yet to find a way of acting as a mediator in such cases. Communication with the herders should be increased, and they should be offered incentives that make it more advantageous for them to comply with land use rules. The conflicts between men and women are due to the unequal rights to acquire and use the donkey carts and so to the PGRN, among others. The project is recommended to apply more flexible subsidization rules with a view to cushioning the disadvantages to which the traditional system of rights exposes women.

In general, the target groups' positive evaluation of the PGRN can be confirmed with the aid of an external view based on a personal appraisal of visible project operations with **transects**. In certain cases, however, the information given by the target groups is qualified by the evaluation team's impression. This is so where the target groups' expectations could not be clearly separated from actual experience, with the result that impacts not expected until some time in the future were described as having already occurred.

Use and potential of MAPP, and its limitations

MAPP takes two days in each village or other social community if the discussion groups are not subdivided. For large programmes, such as the PGRN, it seems appropriate to limit the analysis to a random sample of communities.

An evaluation team of two people is sufficient for MAPP provided that they know the locality and the language and have been trained in the method. Evaluating the data is not very time-consuming, and most of the essential steps are taken by the target group itself. Even illiterate target groups have no difficulty in using the various tools if the evaluation team takes enough time over the introductory discussion and reacts flexibly to the target groups' ideas and abilities.

MAPP pursues the objective of achieving sound and transparent useful results despite its simplicity and relative cheapness. It is for others to decide whether it has been successful in this respect.

MAPP is particularly suitable for use in large programmes with short impact chains. Although MAPP was used here in the context of rural life, there is no reason to believe that it could not be applied to the urban context or in areas other than natural resource management. MAPP still has distinct limitations in the non-systematized recording of general conditions. So far it has, for example, been impossible to make anything more than limited and isolated statements on the vulnerability of social development in the villages concerned, on the prospects for the sustainability of the development achieved and on the time-lag before projects have an impact. These are therefore seen as important areas for the further development of MAPP.

1   Introduction

1.1   The Problem

An evaluation is an attempt to encourage organizations to undertake processes of change on a rational basis by providing them with information on their actions. Accordingly, evaluation research is concerned with the assessment of organizations' activities or of their projects and programmes.[1] In development cooperation evaluation was regarded as the third link in the sequence of the five phases in the project cycle – planning, implementation, evaluation, feedback and replanning – until well into the 1980s. In the meantime a broader view has gained ground, and evaluations are undertaken at virtually any time during the project cycle, i.e. from the "ex ante" stage through the whole project until the "ex post" stage. In technical and human resources cooperation they are no longer used primarily to *monitor* projects but mainly as a management and dialogue tool for all the actors in the development process through and with which "donors and partners" can learn to the benefit of the further progress of the project.

The first concepts for carrying out evaluations emerged in response to the requirements of large government projects and associated capital-intensive growth- and technology-oriented development projects. Initially, this led to a form of evaluation oriented towards economic and technical aspects, which was, moreover, entirely limited to the substance of projects. The societal environment and social issues were not considered.

However, even in the 1970s this view of evaluation was challenged during the debate on the basic needs approach. In a speech he made in Nairobi in 1973 former World Bank President McNamara called for socio-economic standards to be included in development policy and for attention to be focused primarily on the poorest sections of the population (McNamara 1973, pp. 171 ff). At the same time the first academic studies on the operationalization of socio-economic impacts of development projects appeared, Dittmar / Neuhoff (1971), Musto (1972) and Schwefel (1978) being but three examples for the German-speaking world.

It was to be 1980 before the World Bank gave the signal in a publication entitled "*Implementing Programs of Human Development*" (quoted from Salmen 1987) for the **social dimension** to be systematically taken into account in development programmes, and it was to be a further five and seven years, respectively, before the publications "*Putting People First*" (Cernea 1985) and "*Listen to the People*" (Salmen 1987) assigned the target groups in development cooperation an active role from the planning of projects to their evaluation. In Germany the government also began to take a systematic interest in social criteria in the early 1980s. Of importance in this context are the studies commissioned by the Federal Ministry for Economic Development (BMZ) in 1982 and carried out by Ohe and the BMZ's Economic Advisory Council.[2] In the same year the federal government referred in its policy guidelines to the *"growing importance of the social and cultural environment for the effectiveness of development measures"* and called for greater account to be taken of this environment in planning and appraisal.[3]

What practical significance does taking account of the social dimension have, and what aspects need to be considered in its analysis? On the one hand, the socio-cultural framework for development cooperation is singled out for discussion; on the other hand, the focus is on both the social impacts of projects and their socio-economic contents.

In financial cooperation in particular the consideration of social factors is closely associated with the **socio-cultural** aspects. In the early 1980s a start was made on reviewing the socio-cultural requirements for certain projects in the partner country's population. The idea behind this was that a better knowledge of culture – moral concepts in the partner country, for example – would enable it to be considered at an early stage and so improve the prospects for the success of specific development projects. The background to these efforts was formed by previously known evaluation results, according to which a very significant proportion of the failures occurring during the implementation of projects were due to the fact that socio-cultural factors had been ignored.

From the mid-1980s, however, awareness of failures in development grew in the donor countries, and the public increasingly questioned the fundamental purpose of development cooperation. This led initially to general criticism of development policy and eventually, with the growing short-age of financial resources in the donor countries in the 1990s, to the call for a systematic review of the effectiveness of development cooperation in social and development terms. The social dimension is thus taken into account to substantiate the benefits and advantages of development cooperation as such. As the overriding objective of most development projects must be regarded as poverty alleviation, the main aspect of the "effectiveness" of development projects is used to answer the question whether and to what extent they actually help to improve the living conditions of poor sections of the population and so to alleviate poverty. The aim today, however, is not, as it was in the 1970s, to redefine the objectives of development cooperation by again demanding, for example, that aspects of the distribution of welfare among the social strata be taken into account, but rather to ensure the very legitimacy of development cooperation by demonstrating that both absolute and relative poverty in the partner countries is being reduced.

Today all the main development cooperation institutions regard poverty alleviation as a multidimensional task, social criteria being as important as, or even more important than, economic criteria (for example, UNDP 1997). Consequently, an impact analysis designed to reveal the trend in poverty requires not only the established set of economic tools but also a sound social science methodology. Although the scientific approaches devised in the 1970s for the operationalization of social impacts provide initial points of reference for the recording of this phenomenon, the view today is that they are not sufficiently partner-oriented and focus on purely quantitative procedures which no longer conform to the evolving concep-tion of evaluation and are, moreover, too time-consuming and expensive for development organizations to use.[4]

Despite the limited response from practitioners to scientifically sophisti-cated evaluation designs, the tendency for the research community to formulate complex designs continues. Stockmann, for example, has devised a concept with which the sustainability of projects can be evalu-ated. It would cost over DM 100,000 per evaluation, i.e. a mere 15 evaluations of this kind would exhaust the annual budget of the BMZ unit responsible for progress reviews.

On the other hand, the development organizations have yet to systematize the methodological approaches they adopt in evaluation. They often work with simple plausibility statements, without its being at all clear how they are arrived at. What methods are chosen is a question that is frequently not asked at all, or only *en passant*. It is not surprising, then, that it is still considered extremely important *who*, i.e. which institution or consultant, carries out an evaluation. If there was a transparent and valid methodology, what would count most would be *how* the study had been carried out.

It is now an avowed objective of many development organizations to find a methodology for analysing the social impact of projects that requires little effort and yet meets minimum scientific standards.[5] That this demand is being voiced so clearly today is due to the heavy financial and political pressure that is forcing the organizations to reduce their costs while improving the efficiency and quality of their work. For, as Schuster and Pinger, the SPD and CDU/CSU spokesmen on development policy, said in their joint concept for a sustainable development policy in 1998: *"(…) otherwise it will be impossible to maintain, let alone increase, public acceptance of development policy."* (Schuster / Pinger 1998, p. 160)

The search for methods, however, also stems from a professional need felt by cooperation experts to be able to provide information on the impact of their own work. Despite all the criticism of shortcomings, the development sphere occupies a comparatively exemplary position, since its evaluation activity is nowhere near matched by any other sphere.

1.2   Objectives and Structure of the Study

This book is intended as a contribution to the current debate on evaluation methods and specifically to the analysis of the social impact of target-group-oriented development cooperation programmes and projects. It begins by defining the social dimension in development cooperation and describing the *status quo* in the debate on evaluation methods. On the basis of a general chapter devoted to evaluation methodology a method of impact assessment of poverty alleviation projects (MAPP) is developed, tested empirically and assessed. The idea behind MAPP is to give the development organizations a tool for analysing the impact of target-group-oriented programmes and projects that is scientifically sound, easy to use and highly transparent.

This book pursues two objectives of equal value: the theoretical part seeks to provide an overview of the subject matter, while the empirical part describes steps in the operationalization of social impacts that serve to present methods for practical use.

Chapter 2 covers the substantive analysis of the social dimension and clarifies the subject matter of this book. A description of the outline concepts of the World Bank and the Department for International Development (DFID) for the social dimension at macro and meso level is followed by a discussion of the concept for key social processes put forward by the Overseas Development Administration (ODA).[6] The concept can be derived from or underpinned by the outline concepts and is suitable for use at micro level. For MAPP it is used as an evaluation matrix for social impact analysis.

In **Chapter 3** the theoretical and conceptual discussion is temporarily abandoned for a detailed description of the evaluation procedure as currently used by the German development organizations. It is considered whether and how the various organizations take account of the social dimension, what specific objectives they pursue in their evaluation and what strategies and matrices govern their approach to evaluation. This chapter is used to emphasize the practitioners' interest in and need for impact analyses, to reveal methodological shortcomings and to deduce goals for the development of MAPP. The chapter closes by summarizing the most pressing methodological problems connected with evaluation and impact analysis in current practice.

In preparation for the development of MAPP **Chapter 4** considers theoretical evaluation concepts, the change in the conception of evaluation in the research community and the advantages and disadvantages of quantitative versus qualitative procedures. After a goal-oriented discussion of the formation and weighting of indicators conventional and participatory approaches to evaluation are presented, and various methods and tools used to collect data are explained and discussed. The arguments and concepts on which the design of MAPP evaluation is based are identified in this chapter.

On the basis of the concepts presented **Chapter 5** outlines the MAPP method and describes the various tools used. With the aid of a target-group-oriented, sustainable resource management programme in Mali (Projet de Gestion des Ressources Naturelles, PGRN) the method is then put to the test, and the findings are presented and discussed. The chapter ends with an appraisal of the method and an attempt to indicate the potential of MAPP and its limits.

2   The Social Dimension in Development Cooperation

2.1   Definition and Key Aspects of Analysis

"Social" means *"concerning the order of human society"* and refers to the micro and macro levels in a society, i.e. the relationship between individuals, between individuals and groups and between groups within a society.

In development cooperation the social dimension is reflected in all stages of a project and at all levels and is described by Salmen (1987) as follows: *"if time and space be thought of as length and width of a project's fabric, the social dimension may be thought of as its texture."*

According to a World Bank working group set up after the world summit conference on social development held in Copenhagen in 1996, the social dimension is a reference to **people's welfare** and more specifically to their situation and quality of life, their education and the quality and permanence of their institutions and relationships (World Bank 1996, p. 3).

The yardsticks to be used in the evaluation of the social dimension were formulated by the World Bank working group by reference to the objectives adopted in Copenhagen. They are investment in human resources, the creation of employment opportunities and the promotion of democracy, social justice, freedom from violence and equality of opportunity.

The members of the World Bank working group agreed that social development provides the framework for economic development.

In social analysis the development of people, institutions and societies are examined, and the causes of differences in development are analysed. At project level analysis is undertaken to review project strategies for the account they take of individuals and social groups and to determine **who** benefits from projects and strategies and what impacts and risks emanate from them (World Bank 1996, p. 4).

The social dimension does not exist in pure form or as a separate sphere,[1] but overlaps *all* other analytical dimensions of development cooperation[2] or is reflected in other sectors. It is thus a cross-section criterion. At macro level it overlaps in particular the economic, cultural and political dimensions, especially where aspects of social heterogeneity and participation, social capital and organizational development and of political economics, etc. are concerned (see arrows in Figure 1).[3] The social development of people and the quality of life of particularly vulnerable population groups thus depend very largely on the orientation of these factors and so determine the scale of poverty or prosperity in a country.

The **socio-cultural** area of overlapping specifically concerns non-physical aspects that relate to a society's system of values and thought or stand for its cultural identity. In an analysis of these systems in development cooperation the significance of the given socio-culture for the planning of development projects or for the success of a project is considered, as already mentioned above. Important in this context are, for instance, gender issues, the interests of indigenous people and ethnic minorities, problems due to the resettlement of people in the course of project implementation and the question of the participation of target groups in the substance of projects.

The factors in the **socio-economic** area of overlapping, on the other hand, can be physically defined. Economic circumstances are examined, with non-economic variables taken into account.[4] The focus is on the distribution of resources through rights and status or power and macro and sectoral policies and the consequent implications for individual social groups (World Bank 1996, p. 4).

Figure 1:   The social dimension

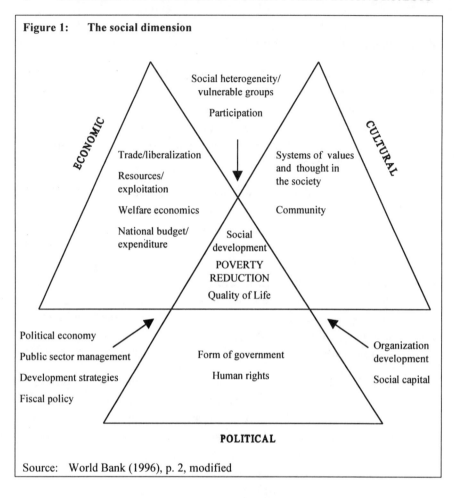

Source: World Bank (1996), p. 2, modified

The issues considered in the **socio-political** area of overlapping concern civil society, respect for human rights and work in countries after wars or other conflicts. On the one hand, the significance and qualities of organizations and institutions are examined, with particular reference to their importance for a country's development. On the other hand, policies that are conducive to development in post-conflict countries or help to prevent conflicts and concern, for example, the reintegration of refugees and former combatants are discussed.

Social analysis focuses on the area in which the dimensions referred to above overlap and interact (see the central triangle in Figure 1). Of particular interest is the poverty orientation of development strategies, country concepts and development projects and their effectiveness in reducing poverty and distributing benefits within the relevant social groups. **Poverty alleviation, social development** and attaining a **better quality of life** can be used as synonyms in development cooperation. The two central questions in social analysis at programme and project level are therefore:

— *Does the programme/project contribute to poverty alleviation?*

— *How are the benefits of the programme/project distributed among the relevant social groups?*

"Poverty" is meant as a multidimensional concept here, as it is currently defined by relevant development institutions and as already shown in Figure 1. The United Nations Development Programme (UNDP), which again modified its concept of poverty in 1997, regards it *as a situation where opportunities and choices most basic to human development are denied – to lead a long, healthy, creative life and to enjoy a decent standard of living, freedom, dignity, self-respect and the respect of others* (UNDP 1997, p. 15).

To operationalize this definition, a concept for social analysis is needed. Recent years have seen some organizations publish concepts and guidelines designed to ensure that account is taken of the social dimension in the development sector. The KfW's concept for target group analysis (1998) and the BMZ's concept for key socio-cultural factors (1992) primarily take account, as the titles themselves indicate, of the socio-cultural aspects of people and target groups and place the emphasis on the legitimacy, i.e. acceptance, of projects.[5] The analysis of the socio-cultural conditions in a region is intended to enable the prospects of development projects succeeding to be assessed with an outline concept that can be operationalized, socio-cultural complexity being subsumed under three key socio-cultural factors. The first of these factors is societal **legitimacy**, which can also be equated with the term *wanting* or acceptance when related to development projects. The second factor is the **level of development** or the *know-how* in the partner country, which might be equated with economic and social competence in a country or region. When this factor is analysed, the compatibility of the initial conditions with the project is considered. The third key factor is the criterion of **socio-cultural heterogeneity**, which coincides with the other two factors. The aim is to determine how socially homogeneous or heterogeneous the society examined is and which relevant social groups dominate and are possibly affected in different ways with respect to the project.

The concept was originally intended for the planning phase of projects and was subsequently declared suitable for use throughout the project cycle and so for impact analysis too (Lachenmann 1988, however). However, the concept is not sufficiently process-oriented for impact analysis and is highly project-related. Furthermore, socio-cultural factors which may have a positive or negative influence on a development cooperation project and are themselves variables capable of being influenced tend to be seen from the evolutionist angle in this outline concept. In the MAPP approach the culturally relativist view tends to be taken, and socio-cultural factors tend to be included as an environmental condition on which little influence can be brought to bear. Nor do they undergo direct evaluation. All in all, the restriction to socio-cultural factors makes this concept unsuitable for a more comprehensive social impact analysis.[6]

Although it is evident that the *"Guidelines for Social Analysis of Development Projects"* published by the Asian Development Bank (ADB, 1993) implicitly take a broader view of the social dimension, the bank makes no attempt to define the term, but focuses on its objectives from the outset. It formulates the effects and requirements that activities *should* have, such as (1) poverty alleviation, (2) consideration of women in the development process, (3) promotion of human resources and (4) prevention of adverse effects of operations on vulnerable groups. These hoped-for effects are not, however, formulated in a clear idea of the social dimension, but simply used as they stand as a yardstick for the evaluation of the bank's activities. The analysis is based on a defined set of questions (Asian Development Bank 1994, pp. 3 ff):

—   definition of the target group: **clientele**;

—   determination of the target group's **needs**;

—   the target group's **demands**;

—   its **absorptive capacity**;

—   **gender issues**;

—   **adverse impact** on highly vulnerable groups.

This package of criteria is also suitable primarily for integration into a project design and thus for the planning phase. In addition, however, the concept provides a framework for monitoring and evaluation, but this framework is highly project-related and not process-oriented. For the individual organization this approach may be appropriate, since it is pragmatic, but as the basis of an overarching method of examining livelihoods it is inadequate.

The only organization that bases its concept on a sound theory and places it in context is the DFID. This institution builds on a comprehensive and structured categorization of a multidimensional concept of poverty and develops the basis for the conceptual recording of social development. In 1995 it offered a matrix for recording the social dimension at micro level, which is explained in the next section and will be operationalized with the help of MAPP in the last chapter of this study. In addition to the existing definition of key social factors, however, the DFID's Natural Resources Policy and Advisory Department (NRPAD) set up in 1997 an interinstitutional working group, which is developing a concept for **sustainable rural livelihoods (SRL)** that may underpin the existing matrix conceptually. Although the SRL concept has yet to be completed and is therefore fragmentary in places, it includes some interesting points of departure, which will be explained below.[7]

The working group is considering the term "livelihood" in a rural context. In principle it assumes that, besides the early improvement of an individual's livelihood, the management of natural resources needs to be improved if poverty is to be alleviated in the longer term. On this basis, which also takes account of the aspect of finitely available environmental resources, yet places human beings at the centre, the following definition of SRL is proposed:

> *"A livelihood comprises the capabilities, assets (including both material and social resources) and activities required for a means of living. A livelihood is sustainable when it can cope*

with and recover from stresses and shocks and maintain or en-
hance its capabilities and assets both now and in the future,
while not undermining the natural resource base. "

This definition is highly consistent with UNDP's definition of poverty, although the organizations emphasize different aspects. While UNDP places greater emphasis on human rights, human dignity and freedom, the DFID attaches greater importance to sustainability in that it analyses the vulnerability or buffer capacities associated with any quality of life that has been achieved. And these are related closely to finite environmental resources. The outline concept that builds on this definition now pursues the following goals:

— The definitional range of SRL is to be unambiguous and form a basis for the analysis of SRL,

— the complexity of rural life is to become more comprehensible with the help of the outline concept,

— the concept is to act as a frame of reference for anyone concerned with rural development and SRL analyses,

— it is to be a starting point for the formulation of medium-term objectives with a view to improving people's livelihoods.

The concept is based on work by the Institute of Development Studies (IDS) and proceeds from a holistic and process-oriented view that takes account of the complexity of poverty and development. Besides seeking to be easily understood and as widely accepted as possible, it is highly practical. The working group also attempts to identify links between the micro and macro levels with the help of the concept.

The outline concept pivots on the idea that people's livelihoods can be explained by reference to five different types of assets, upon which individuals draw to build their livelihoods. These are:

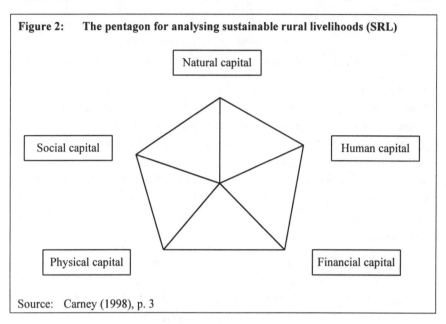

Figure 2:   The pentagon for analysing sustainable rural livelihoods (SRL)

Natural capital

Social capital

Human capital

Physical capital

Financial capital

Source: Carney (1998), p. 3

The five types of assets can be described as follows:

Natural capital: Reserves of natural resources that benefit people (e.g. land, water, biodiversity, environmental resources)

Human capital: Competence and know-how. Ability to work and sufficiently good health to enable different life strategies to be pursued

Social capital: Social resources with which people shape their lives and pursue objectives (e.g. networks, membership of groups, relationships based on trust, access to institutions)

Physical capital: Basic infrastructure (e.g. transport, housing, water, energy, communications) and an endowment with means of production that enables people to shape their lives

Financial capital: Available financial resources that give people various options in their lives (e.g. assets, access to credits, regular income, income from investment)

The different types of assets are presented schematically as a pentagon. This is a five-axis graph on which access by different groups or households to each different type of asset can be plotted. This concept does not include an absolute poverty line or define a point above which people have, for example, an adequate and sustainable livelihood. For the assessment of livelihood, according to the DFID, achieving absolute values with respect to a given factor is less important than the volume above (or below) the pentagon that occurs when all the various values are entered and linked.

The plotting of such pentagons enables people's livelihoods to be appraised, but a second step needs to be taken to enable statements on sustainability to be made. Thus once the first step of defining the current position, as it were, has been taken, the second step is to ask how livelihoods have changed in the past, what trends are emerging and what is responsible for any change that has occurred.

In this qualitative analysis it is essential to consider the **general conditions** that affect the **vulnerability** of SRLs which have been achieved and so may result in a situation where even pentagons with identical patterns differ in significance. Such general conditions are not only a country's political and economic conditions but also such aspects as the level of technology, population growth, the climate, the socio-culture and conflicts in a society. It is also important to understand the society's structures and processes, since they help to determine people's **options in life**. They include the structure of organizations and sectors, existing legislation, economic incentives and rules relating to social life. These structures can influence livelihoods in two ways:

1.   Structures influence the importance of a gain in assets for different people and social groups and determine the *effective value* of the gain in a given type of capital.

2. In conjunction with people's existing financial situations structures also have a bearing on access to types of assets and the types that are particularly attractive.

Markets and legal restrictions also have a profound influence on the extent to which one asset can be converted into another type of asset. The goal should be equal convertibility of all types, since this increases the options in life and the means of compensating for stresses and shocks. At the second step of the SRL analysis an attempt is therefore made to build a bridge between the macro and micro levels.

On the basis of this conception the DFID now formulates objectives which are to be achieved in the medium term and which guide the DFID's work:

— assured access to and improved management of natural resources,

— a supportive social environment with good cohesion,

— improved access to high-quality education and training, information, technology, food and health,

— improved access to facilitating infrastructure,

— a political and institutional environment which makes different blueprints for life possible and in which the goal is equal access to competitive markets.

The third step, which is important primarily for programme planning, consists in adding a qualitative analysis of effectiveness, in which the partner and the development cooperation mediators are involved. The question to be answered is which type of asset lies within the DFID's and its partner's sphere of influence for a contribution to the reduction of poverty and which of these spheres seems most productive in terms of goal achievement. For this the DFID is planning to establish indicators, which are to be adopted in a process of dialogue with the counterpart organization or target groups.

The design for the DFID's outline concept ends with this step. The approach seems comprehensive, plausible, context-related and process-oriented. Depicting livelihoods as pentagons is reminiscent of the development diamonds which have been used in the World Bank's social development statistics since 1994 and with the aid of which the four social indicators *"average life expectancy, school enrolment rate, access to drinking water and gross domestic product per capita"* are related to one another at macro level (World Bank 1994a).

The working group itself sees the greatest advantage of the outline concept in its being holistic and abandoning sectoral thinking. It sees the fact that its concept takes account of the sustainability aspect as a component of the quality of life as an inconsistency. According to the working group, the concept is inconsistent with the generally accepted view that for extremely poor people in particular successful strategies for survival in the short term have priority over the sustainable management of natural resources. Nonetheless, the working party stands by its decision to include this aspect on the grounds that it clearly helps the people concerned to maintain an improved livelihood and is therefore very important (Carney 1998, p. 5).

The concept developed is a framework for the analysis of people's livelihoods and makes it easier for intermediate objectives to be set for the work of development organizations. It focuses on people and forges a link between the micro and macro levels. However, the outline concept does not formulate any indicators or yardsticks for defining positions on the pentagon and therefore remains very abstract. In 1995 the DFID put forward a more concrete concept, which can be deduced without difficulty from the outline concept and is, conversely, underpinned by it.

2.2   The Concept of the ODA's Key Social Processes

In the concept of key social processes the ODA begins by assuming that all development projects form an integral part of a society and, as society does not function statically but dynamically, contribute to social change to a greater or lesser degree. The aim of a social analysis is to find out whether the direction taken with this change is consistent with the objectives of projects. In a contextual impact analysis, on the other hand, it is asked whether and to what extent the identified social changes can be attributed to the work of the project. To identify social changes, four dichotomized key processes under which, according to the ODA, all relevant social categories can be subsumed are defined (ODA 1995, pp. 35 ff):

— **livelihoods:** improvement or impoverishment
  (e.g. level and security of income, nutritional status, consumption, agricultural yields, health, school meals, etc.),

— **resources:** access or exclusion
  (e.g. access to water, wood, land, credits, markets, information and work),

— **knowledge:** expansion or reduction
  (e.g. traditional know-how, knowledge acquired at school, literacy, know-how acquired from the project context),

— **rights:** participation or alienation
  (in and outside the project structure, e.g. decision-making powers, participatory rights, land rights, conflicts).

For a social analysis the ODA believes that the trends in these key processes as they relate to all relevant social groups differentiated, for example, by gender, religion, ethnic background, social strata, etc. should be examined separately.

The four key processes represent the DFID's pentagon of assets in concrete terms. In the case of the key processes, however, different forms of resources (e.g. access to infrastructure or to land) are entered under the same generic heading. This is substantively of no importance in an impact analysis, however. While the DFID's types of assets are couched in neutral terms, the key processes contain a normative element that points in the direction which can be rated positive or negative. This enables the key processes to be dichotomized, which makes them tangible and assessable. They thus become a suitable basis for pursuing operationalization with scales, for example.

As Table 1 shows, the four key processes at micro level are subsumed into the five types of assets or can be completely transposed to them. Another advantage of using the key processes as the starting point for operationalization is that the designations are far more easily and spontaneously understood. The conceptual shell of "asset or capital" for all sides

Table 1:   The DFID's outline concept for the social dimension and the ODA's key social processes

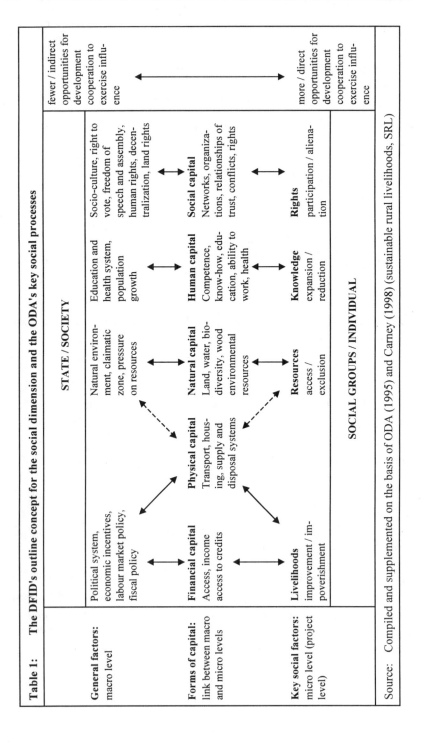

STATE / SOCIETY

SOCIAL GROUPS / INDIVIDUAL

fewer / indirect opportunities for development cooperation to exercise influence

more / direct opportunities for development cooperation to exercise influence

General factors: macro level

Political system, economic incentives, labour market policy, fiscal policy

Natural environment, claimatic zone, pressure on resources

Education and health system, population growth

Socio-culture, right to vote, freedom of speech and assembly, human rights, decentralization, land rights

Forms of capital: link between macro and micro levels

Financial capital Access, income access to credits

Physical capital Transport, housing, supply and disposal systems

Natural capital Land, water, biodiversity, wood environmental resources

Human capital Competence, know-how, education, ability to work, health

Social capital Networks, organizations, relationships of trust, conflicts, rights

Key social factors: micro level (project level)

Livelihoods improvement / impoverishment

Resources access / exclusion

Knowledge expansion / reduction

Rights participation / alienation

Source: Compiled and supplemented on the basis of ODA (1995) and Carney (1998) (sustainable rural livelihoods, SRL)

of the pentagon also suggests that all the criteria are physical, i.e. they can be *acquired, owned* and *consumed*, whereas the aspects of active learning, developing, co-existing and participating are lost or placed on an economic basis through the use of the term "capital". This is compatible with the thinking of western socio-culture, but might easily lead to misunderstandings in many other societies.

The ODA further differentiates the four key processes by sectors by proposing in each case a check list with subcategories for carrying out social analyses.[8] Unlike the concepts of other organizations, which are highly project-related in their very approach, both the DFID pentagon and the ODA key processes are context-related, and the ODA criteria are also highly target-group-oriented. The dichotomization of the criteria focuses attention on the dynamism of social processes, which is vital in project evaluation. The criteria can be used both as a guide frame for recording the initial situation and for monitoring throughout the project cycle.

While the four key processes are suitable for further operationalization at project level, the SRL approach ensures that the link to the macro level is not lost. The two approaches are therefore to be seen as complementing each other. At methodological level, however, no further progress is made with the two concepts.[9] Although a participatory approach is explicitly advocated in both cases, neither comments on the systematic collection and evaluation of data for a social impact analysis. This is where MAPP comes in.

Gsänger and Voipio (1997) took the first conceptual step towards improving the comparability of the findings on the basis of the ODA matrix by basing it on a scale of one to five (see Table 2). Although they do not discuss the method of collecting data and do not fill the matrix with empirical data, they do give a first impression of how evaluation findings can be presented in an illustrative, informative and compact form, with comparability ensured. In the empirical part of this study a simplified form of such a matrix tailored to natural resource management is adopted for evaluation in social impact analysis.

Table 2:   Modified matrix of the key social processes

	Livelihoods Improvement	Resources Access	Knowledge Expansion	Rights participation	Impact
Sub-categories	Income — Consumption — Employment — Nutrition — Health — Security — Markets — Shelter	Land tenure — Extension service — Health service — Technology — Transportation — Safety nets — Communications — Credit	Children's schooling — Adult literacy — Skills — Indigenous knowledge used	Ownership rights — Gender equality — Partipation — Self reliance — Speech — Empowerment	
					++ Very positive
					+ Positive
					+/- No change
					- Negative
					-- Very negative
	Impoverishment	Exclusion	Reduction	Alienation	

Source: Gsänger / Viopio (1997), modified in accordance with ODA

3   Taking Account of the Social Dimension in Evaluation

3.1   The Evaluation Procedure

3.1.1   Evaluation Objectives and Definitions

According to the guidelines of the Expert Group on Aid Evaluation set up by the OECD's Development Assistance Committee (DAC), *an evaluation is an assessment, as systematic and objective as possible, of an on-going or completed project, programme or policy, its design, implementation and results. The aim is to determine the relevance and fulfilment of objectives, developmental efficiency, effectiveness, impact and sustainability. An evaluation should provide information that is credible and useful, enabling the incorporation of lessons learned into the decision-making process of both recipients and donors* (DAC 1992, p. 132).

In practice, this lofty and comprehensive ambition of the DAC for evaluations is rarely fulfilled. While the criterion of **effectiveness** or review of the degree of goal achievement (target-performance comparison) is usually fairly easy to evaluate, the first serious difficulties arise as a rule when an attempt is made to assess **efficiency**, since it often appears impossible to express actual benefits in money terms. Approaches to overcoming these difficulties are cost-benefit calculations, the analysis of cost-effectiveness and the establishment of project-specific efficiency indicators that enable the efficiency of one project to be related to that of similar projects. Another approach is to calculate the benefit subjectively perceived by the target group and to compare it to the costs caused by the project.

By definition, the **sustainability** of a project can be determined only in ex post analyses. By that time, however, negative results can no longer be corrected. It is therefore equally important to carry out an evaluation during or before project implementation to see whether the conditions that permit or promote sustainability have been taken into account in the planning or require adjustment. What these conditions are depends on the concept of sustainability, on which views may differ widely. In principle, the question that is always asked when a project is examined for sustainability is whether the benefits will be sustainably enjoyed by the target groups. An added complication is that expectations as to the nature of these benefits have changed considerably in recent years. Initially, a highly project-oriented view dominated, and sustainability was deemed to exist where a target group continued with an innovation in its own interests and by its own efforts. According to a broader, output- or production-oriented definition, sustainability exists only where the target group or sponsor has a structure that enables them sustainably to derive benefits for others as well as themselves. UNDP takes a system-oriented view and is even more ambitious: a project is deemed to be sustainable only if diffusion processes have resulted in an improvement in the performance of the whole system. Another view, the most ambitious of the definitions, also means that sustainable projects must have developed in the target group or counterpart organization a potential for innovation that enables them to react flexibly to other environmental conditions.[1]

Definitions of sustainability that go beyond the individual project can also be equated with the concept of sustained effectiveness and so overlap the concept of **significance**. A project is described as significant if it has a broad sectoral or regional impact, contributes to the formation of structures or, being of a model nature, can be replicated in other sectors or regions. Although concepts relating to structure-forming effects can no longer be clearly distinguished from one another, the two criteria of "sustainability" and "broad impact" are not infrequently seen as opposites, since some evaluations have shown projects to be sustainable particularly when they are small and modest in design (Hillebrand / Messner / Meyer-Stamer 1993, pp. 26 f.; Kohlmann 1998). Where a system-oriented concept of sustainability is taken as the basis, however, they then satisfy only some of the sustainability criteria.

The criteria for reviewing the **effects** (= **impacts**) of a project usually relate to overriding objectives which describe, for example, the social benefits to the people concerned or the effectiveness of the project in development terms. Even though impact has now been integrated into the DAC guidelines as an examination criterion, impact analyses have hitherto been carried out rarely or very inadequately owing to the lack of suitable concepts (Mohs 1997). Instead, impact analyses are often no more than investigations which do not extend beyond the project limits and in which the achievement of project objectives is equated with supposed impacts of the project.

Those active in the development field today use a wide range of terms for evaluations. The choice of term depends both on the development institution and its functions and interests and on differing traditions, approaches and regional linguistic usage. In **governmental development cooperation** the BMZ used the term "evaluation" until a few years ago because it was linked to a review by external experts. This is now known as **external evaluation**. The BMZ's evaluations unit was renamed the Progress Review Department some years ago, having originally been known as the Inspection Department. According to an HWWA definition, a progress review covers all activities relating to the continuous observation and documentation of the activities of current projects (monitoring) and the periodic evaluation of the success of current and completed projects (Borrmann et al. 1998, p. 3). The KfW also uses this term for its set of evaluation tools. For all evaluations carried out by governmental implementing organizations themselves, on the other hand, other terms are used. They are **self-evaluations**, some of which are conducted by external experts (= internal third-party evaluations) and which in their entirety form an internal reporting system partly geared to the BMZ.

Usage differs in the case of the **non-governmental organizations** (NGOs), which generally refer to evaluations even when they are not normally comprehensive evaluations as defined in the DAC guidelines but partial evaluations, i.e. the appraisal of certain aspects. Given their smaller budgets and their structure, NGOs do not as a rule have a set of tools for project planning and evaluation comparable to those of governmental organizations. Nor, owing to their size and, to some extent, their beliefs and background, do they always have evaluation departments.

Effectiveness or **impact analysis** corresponds to **impact evaluation** or sometimes to a review of the overall goal. While effectiveness analysis is guided by objectives and asks whether they have had an impact on the project environment or the target group, impact analysis considers both effects that conform to the objectives of the project and effects that do not do so. A **social impact analysis** can be equated with a poverty impact evaluation provided that the latter is based on a multidimensional definition of poverty and pays equal attention to social criteria as defined by UNDP.

Evaluations of the overall goal are traditionally carried out by the BMZ, but some are undertaken by the KfW. Reviews of the overall goal by the BMZ are political in nature. Depending on the objectives formulated, they correspond to the evaluation of project **effectiveness in development terms**, which covers both political and strategic objectives. The KfW links the evaluation of effectiveness in development terms to the preparation of the final report that is produced on every project after its "completion" (for further information see section 3.2.2).

Terms related to "evaluation" are "appraisal" and "monitoring". The term **appraisal** is frequently used for ex ante evaluations. Precise distinctions do not, however, correspond to practical usage. **Monitoring** was long taken to mean a continuous process of observation during the implementation of a project, in contrast to evaluation. Since many organizations began to see evaluation as process-oriented, the two terms have come closer together in meaning. Until a few years ago, however, a clear distinction was made to the extent that monitoring was internal to the project, whereas evaluations were made by external consultants. This distinction too is currently becoming less clear, since evaluations are more and more often carried out by the counterpart himself.

From these explanations it is clear that the use of different terms for evaluations is not only due to the different functions of development institutions, but is also accompanied by a changing conception of the process and objectives of evaluation and overall policy. By and large, governmental and non-governmental organizations are converging in their ideas in this context. The institutional differences that continue to find expression in some areas of evaluation will be discussed in the following.

An innovation at the **GTZ** is, for example, the use of the **client-oriented quality concept** (Klaus 1998; Steigerwald 1998). The choice of this term corresponds to the GTZ's self-image as a service enterprise that gears its "products" to the needs of "clients". It is therefore assumed that it is the client who decides whether the product is good or bad and whether he wants to go on using it. This subjectivist quality concept thus rates as good what the client considers to be good. This means that responsibility for evaluations tends to be shifted to the partner organization. The result is **"open" impact observation** in which the utmost importance is attached to evaluation by the client.[2] The GTZ is thus increasingly interested in ex ante evaluations undertaken during the project by its own staff and with the participation of the target group. Only then can evaluation findings be of direct benefit to institutional learning and used as guidance or management tools. This trend has also been apparent in non-governmental organizations for some time. They regard evaluation primarily as a participatory management tool used principally to achieve the goal of joint learning during project implementation.

For the **BMZ**, on the other hand, an evaluation must also perform other important functions. The institution must know whether certain strategies have been "worthwhile" and whether programmes and projects are ultimately successful, and it must be possible to explain to the public their success (or failure) as compared to other policies. The BMZ is therefore interested in knowing whether programmes are sustainable, have a broad impact and can ultimately be rated positive or negative. In other words, it is particularly interested in **ex post evaluations**. For the KfW too ex post analyses are of the utmost importance. This is due both to the difference in its concept of project from the GTZ's, the KfW placing the emphasis on the "provision" of economic or social infrastructure, a project thus being deemed to have been "completed" once this has been done, and to the fact that the KfW does not employ any long-term experts locally. This undoubtedly increases the need for greater emphasis to be placed on the supervisory aspect of evaluations.

The **counterpart organizations** in the partner countries have different interests again where evaluation is concerned. They often have reservations about evaluation, because they fear that it may be associated with negative budgetary decisions. It is therefore a very rare occurrence for evaluation to be initiated by a partner. This explains the counterparts' interest during the evaluation in gaining more control over the evaluation process and the evaluation findings, in strengthening their own evaluation capacities and in placing even greater emphasis on the process of learning from evaluations than the GTZ and many non-governmental organizations already do.

As the explanations show, despite the convergence of views within the various organizations on what constitutes evaluation, there continue to be major differences, which can be attributed to the background and working methods of the various organizations and the functions they perform in development cooperation. Besides these characteristics, which clearly stand in the way of standardization, the conception of evaluation has generally changed in recent decades owing in part to changes in evaluation research, and this in turn has had repercussions for the organizations at different speeds and intensities (see section 4.2).

3.1.2   Types of Evaluation and Composition of the Evaluation Team

Evaluations can not only be undertaken at different times during the project cycle by teams of varying composition: they can also be related to different sectors, types of project or countries.[3] In any evaluation covering more than one project it is important for the findings to be comparable. A lack of comparability due to existing methodological shortcomings has serious implications in this respect.

The following diagram shows the various types of evaluation used by the BMZ. To compare the hierarchy of objectives with the actual situation, use is made of the indicators on the horizontal axis, where there are three categories: **monitoring**, **self-evaluation** and **third-party evaluation**, which passes from the question *"whether what is being done is being done right"* to a higher level of objectives and the question *"whether the right thing is being done."* (Breier 1998b, p. 128)

Hitherto the BMZ has usually carried out all forms of evaluation as "external third-party evaluations", while monitoring, target-performance comparisons, progress reviews and "internal third-party evaluations" have been undertaken on the implementing organizations' own initiative (see Annex 1). In governmental cooperation a distinction can also be made in accordance with the following criteria:

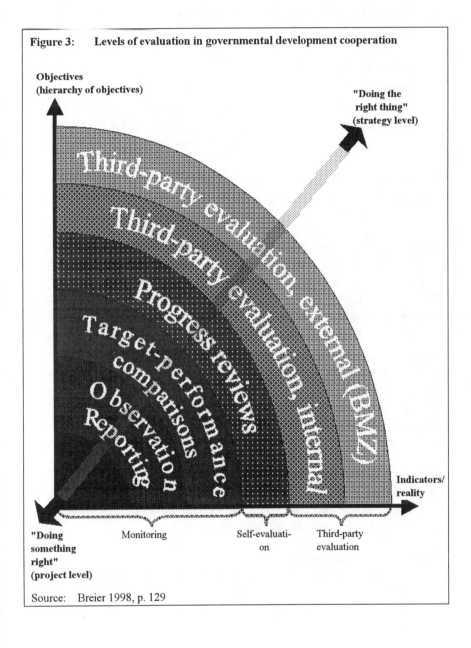

Figure 3:   Levels of evaluation in governmental development cooperation

Source: Breier 1998, p. 129

— **Reporting and (unsystematic) observation**
 The reports are based on missions, reports in the media and from em-
 bassies, etc., discussions during government negotiations with partner countries, etc.

— **Internal and systematic progress review**
 The reviews are undertaken by the various institutions with the help,
 for example, of an M&E system and are supplemented by purposeful,
 systematic reviews by the work units managing the project (see section 3.2.3).

— **External progress review**
 External reviews by audit firms, the BMZ, or experts engaged by the
 BMZ, or the Federal Audit Office.

Another way of distinguishing evaluations is to consider the different
types of project. For impact evaluations in particular a highly relevant
factor is the length of the impact chains between the "service" and the
"end user" of the service. Another term used in this context is the project's
"direct and indirect link to poverty". As, for example, policy advice
projects, whose importance is growing in technical cooperation, have very
long impact chains until they are able to have an impact on target groups,
they are very difficult to evaluate in this respect. Projects geared to very
practical measures (e.g. infrastructure projects in financial cooperation)
and grass-roots projects, which address the target group itself, have short
impact chains, cause-and-effect relationships being far easier to identify
in the latter case.

However, evaluations can also be distinguished in terms of who carries
out the examination, i.e. individual consultants or a team, external or
internal experts, project staff, with the participation of the target group or
by the partner organization entirely on its own.

(1) **External consultants**
 External consultants are employed on the BMZ's "external" evaluations. They are commissioned by the BMZ and carry out evaluations
 in accordance with the BMZ's terms of reference (ToR) and its
 evaluation list.

(2) **Joint evaluation**
In a joint evaluation different types of actors, i.e. various implementing organizations, target groups and assisting organizations, are represented in the evaluation team.

(3) **Self-evaluation**
This is internal evaluation by the implementing organization, but it may also be carried out by internal third parties. However, self-evaluation often means activities of the counterpart organizations which they can initiate and undertake autonomously, but which may well include external advice.

The change in the conception of evaluation is also associated with a change in the role of the evaluator team. The roles of *technician, researcher, monitor* and *assessor* which the evaluator has hitherto ideally played are increasingly being joined today by the roles of *collaborator, moderator* and *manager*. Instead of being, at best, an instrument for change through the submission of findings of an extractive examination that uncovers problems, the evaluator required by many organizations today tends to prompt change himself on the basis of results arrived at jointly (Kasch 1997).

When the numerous forms of evaluation and the wide range of actors who may be involved in an evaluation are considered, it becomes clear that there cannot be *one ideal* evaluation method. Rather there is a need to choose the best method for the type, purpose and time concerned or to modify a method to suit the circumstances. However, an outline concept that could be adjusted flexibly to prevailing requirements – through the inclusion of specific elements, for example – might conceivably be developed.

3.2   Evaluation in Germany

Evaluations in German development cooperation are carried out by the BMZ and the implementing organizations, by political foundations, the Churches, non-governmental organizations, audit firms and the Federal

Audit Office. The leading actors in evaluation also include the many freelance consultants working for the various organizations.

The BMZ and the various organizations have guidelines or rules on how to carry out an evaluation. Even though the organizations gear evaluations to the specific features of their approaches, a logical framework continues to be the basic methodological tool used by almost all organizations. They seek to determine whether targets have been achieved by the project activities. The ToR and the organization's own specific evaluation list are then used as the basis for carrying out the evaluation. Besides question-naires to be completed using set indicators, the ToR contain information on the composition of the evaluation team and on the preferred or possi-ble methodology. What the ToR do not say, on the other hand, is how the data collected are to be reflected in the evaluation report or on which concept and impact model the evaluation is to be based. As a concept of this kind usually exists no more than implicitly anywhere in evaluation in development cooperation, the data collected tend to be processed intui-tively rather than systematically. Ideally, an evaluation report contains answers to the questions posed in the ToR and information in its annex. It should be drawn up not by one individual but by the team and, if possible, discussed by a larger group on the spot.

The rules on the **feedback of evaluation findings** into the project cycle or overriding cooperation concepts depend on the organization. While the KfW and GTZ have clear prescriptions, smaller organizations decide on each case as it arises. It would be an advantage, however, if, at the time they agreed to undertake an evaluation, the organizations concerned adopted a set of rules on the form to be taken by follow-up measures, since experience shows that there is otherwise a grave danger of no use whatever being made of the findings (see section 4.2).

As the BMZ sees it, it would be a welcome advance if evaluation was more closely coordinated – with the implementing organizations, includ-ing the NGOs – thus enabling harmonization and better comparability to be achieved even in the evaluation of jointly financed projects. With a view to pooling existing knowledge of German evaluation and making it accessible to all institutions, the BMZ has commissioned the Hamburg Institute for Economic Research (HWWA) to evaluate German evaluation activity.[4] This is intended to lead to greater coherence, to less duplication of effort and to synergies through interinstitutional learning.

In the following sections of this study the evaluation activities of the most important German actors will be considered, but with a more specific goal than that pursued by the HWWA: to identify the methodological approaches of the various actors and to analyse how they take account of the social dimension and record the impacts of projects. At the end of the chapter the results of this appraisal will be summarized, and the main problems, most of them methodological, will be described through the actors' eyes and commented on.

3.2.1   Evaluation by the BMZ

The BMZ's Progress Review Department at present carries out some 50 - 60 evaluations each year, covering about 1.5 - 2 % of current projects. The reviews are meant to be comprehensive, systematic and critical investigations in which account is taken of all essential aspects in technical and development terms.

The social dimension is considered in all BMZ evaluations on the basis of different outline concepts. Concepts exist both for the key sociocultural factors and achieving gender equality and for poverty orientation in projects (BMZ 1988; 1990a; 1990b; 1992; 1995). The various criteria are covered in the evaluations by reference to an evaluation list,[5] which takes the form of a target-performance comparison geared to the project objective. This covers many social aspects, which are listed under various points in the evaluation list.

As there are no instructions or guidelines at the BMZ on how the consultants are to process the list, i.e. on how they should collect and evaluate data, they largely decide for themselves. Whether they undertake target group analyses and how they do so is also left to them or is specified in the ToR during preliminary discussions. This results in there being a **wide range of approaches** to evaluation, which is almost impossible to grasp and which also seems haphazard. Consequently, evaluation findings are often very difficult to compare.

Evaluation by the BMZ and its structure have, however, been reoriented in recent months (Breier 1998b, p. 129). The Ministry has assigned more of the responsibility for evaluation to the implementing organizations so that it may concentrate more on central and strategic tasks in the conceptual formulation of evaluation policy and so improve the quality of and approaches to evaluation.[6] Greater emphasis is to be placed in particular on thematic, sectoral and instrument evaluations in the future. Most of these "strategic" evaluations will, however, continue to be based on random samples composed of individual development projects. Where an individual evaluation of this kind does not form part of a random sample, it will be carried out by the implementing organizations themselves in the future.

The evaluation department has defined its reorientation in its two-year evaluation programme for 1998/99. With the assistance of experts evaluations relating in particular to the sustainability of financial and technical cooperation projects are to be carried out. The appropriate department is not saying anything definite about its future publication policy, which has hitherto been very restrictive, i.e. evaluation reports may not be inspected by outsiders.[7] The first step to easing this policy will probably consist in making selected evaluations or chapters accessible to the public in the future.[8]

The BMZ does not explicitly emphasize the participatory aspect in evaluations. The partners' own interest in the evaluation of projects is currently rated low, and the openness they can be expected to show is regarded as limited because of their interest in obtaining funds. A rather restrained attitude towards the partners' participation is also due to the strategic orientation of BMZ evaluation on institutional grounds. It would seem difficult, however, to maintain this position, especially when it comes to ex post appraisals of projects handed over to partners.

3.2.2   Evaluation by the KfW

The KfW monitors all its projects and conducts its own evaluations, which take account of every stage of the project cycle, but focus on ex post analyses.[9] During the project appraisal phase the KfW undertakes forward-looking analyses and assessments, which cover many economic and institutional aspects and also contain socio-economic and socio-cultural forecasts. The acceptance of projects by the people is regarded as vital in this context (KfW 1992, pp. 23 ff.) It is assessed in advance with the target group analysis, which is based on the BMZ's outline concept for key socio-cultural factors (BMZ 1990a; Bliss / Gaesing / Neumann 1997). With the aid of a three-stage analytical technique this enables a project's "social success risks" to be determined. The purpose of the analysis is to increase the compatibility of the project with the users' interests while avoiding adverse effects or to establish compensatory plans (KfW 1998b, pp. 1-11).

The **target group analysis** consists of three processing stages: the **plausibility check** begins with an assessment of the composition of the target groups, the expected acceptance of the project, the legitimacy of its counterpart organization, potential impacts and the coping capacity of the target and other population groups. The appraisal does not presuppose an "on-the-spot inspection", but is based on an analysis of secondary sources. If the plausibility check shows there to be major shortages of information or the success of the project to be at serious risk, further analyses, i.e. a brief local analysis or an analysis of the potential social impact, are added. Otherwise, the termination of this first stage marks the end of the target group analysis.

The **brief local analysis** is a local check that helps to avoid or emphasizes the need for more extensive inquiries. It is used to uncover "social success risks" (e.g. potential opposition from or marginalization of population groups) and constitutes a more detailed plausibility check. The data are based on interviews with key informants, the KfW staff's own observations in the project area and secondary information. Interviews with the target groups are not sought.

If doubts concerning the "social success risks" cannot be eliminated by the brief analysis, an **analysis of potential social impact** is now added. The aim is both to conduct a more detailed analysis of the social context and potential effects of the project and to identify the consequences. The analysis takes from two to four months and includes comprehensive and systematic interviews or consultation with the various target groups. It may also include proposals for contractual agreements with the partner and suggestions for compensatory strategies or changes of location. The participation of the target groups in the formulation of these proposals is possible, but not mandatory in this context.

When a project reaches the implementation phase, the KfW has another three tools for reviewing progress (KfW 1997a, pp. 18-42). At at least yearly intervals **progress review reports** are forwarded to the federal government with a model breakdown. They are drawn up locally under the supervision of experts and contain target-performance comparisons. On the completion of the investment phase a **final follow-up**, which is guided by the structure of the project appraisal report and also represents, in essence, a technical and financial target-performance comparison, takes place. However, if it is clear at this time that environmental or socio-cultural aspects are having seriously adverse effects on the running of the project or if the sustainability of the project does not appear to be ensured, the problems are considered at this stage and solutions are proposed.

Three to five years after each project is completed a **final local evalua-tion** is carried out. Actual and target values are compared, and it is considered what conclusions can be drawn for the implementation of similar projects (lessons learnt). Depending on the type of project, differentiated statements on the effects on the people have to be made at the time of the final evaluation. The findings in the final reports include an assessment of each project's "effectiveness in development terms", which is aligned with the assessment of independent auditors.

In the evaluation of **effectiveness in development terms** account is taken of general sectoral factors, the achievement of project objectives, micro-economic profitability, macroeconomic effects, socio-economic and social-cultural impacts, environmental impacts and an assessment of the prospects for sustainability.[10]

To identify the socio-economic impacts, questions are asked about the implications of the project for the lives of the various target groups. A set list of criteria is not available for this, however; instead, the impacts are "identified" by inference through the appraisal of technical and economic data (e.g. data on the use of drinking water facilities) or secondary sources (e.g. statistics on epidemics). As a rule they thus represent an assessment by experts in which the subjective views of the target group and its judgment on the distribution of benefits play no part.

The overall appraisal of the effectiveness of a project in development terms is finally made on the basis of the various findings with the aid of a six-point rating scale from "highly effective" to "total failure". How the various factors are weighted is decided on a case-by-case basis and is not transparent (cf. KfW 1997b, pp. 92-96).

3.2.3   Evaluation by the GTZ

To enable the findings to be immediately reflected in management measures, the GTZ's evaluations are mainly carried out during the project implementation phase as part of "Monitoring & Evaluation" (M&E) and "Project Progress Reviews" (PPRs). The organization considers ex post analyses appropriate only in exemplary individual cases. It prefers **self-evaluation**, since its experience shows this to have the strongest learning effects, and operations and plans can immediately reflect any insights gained.

For the GTZ **monitoring** has hitherto meant the systematic observation and documentation of project implementation on the basis of planning. In recent years, however, the conception of M&E has evolved, the focus increasingly shifting to the process of negotiation among all concerned in a project, with the emphasis on reflection and understanding within the team and the goal being a continuous improvement in the quality of projects through these communication processes (GTZ 1992; 1997a, p. 6).

While the significance and impacts of project activities were hardly relevant as M&E was once understood, these levels are included in the modern conception. With what is known as **utilization monitoring** the actual use made by the target group of the services offered is determined, and with **impact monitoring** the correctness of the basic development hypothesis is examined. In the monitoring of cooperative relations greater attention is paid to the development of relations between the partners, and the aim in **context monitoring** is to identify the social, economic, political and, possibly, locational changes and tendencies relevant to the project. If this new conception is actually implemented, modern M&E has a sufficiently wide frame to embrace the evaluation of the social dimension during project implementation.

Unlike M&E, which is carried out continuously and by project staff, **PPRs** are undertaken periodically, i.e. every two to four years, and by third parties unconnected with the project in accordance with a binding GTZ guide. A Project Progress Review is defined as *"... a systematic examination of the planning, implementation and impacts of a technical cooperation project or programme, with account taken of all aspects of relevance in development and technical terms."* As a rule, it is requested only when fundamental decisions on project implementation are about to be taken ("milestones" in the project cycle) (GTZ 1991, p. 2). A PPR essentially consists of target-performance comparisons, and explanations are given and recommendations made in respect of any deviations. The findings and evaluations emerging from a review of this kind are included in the preparation of any subsequent project phase as an important information base.

Although a PPR check list contains numerous questions relating to the social dimension, target group orientation, participation, the account taken of women and self-help aspects, the review focuses on the evaluation of the operation of the project in accordance with the planning specifications. Given the close link to the project, the level of the project objectives, let alone overall goals, is seldom reached and questioned during a PPR, even though the option theoretically exists (see, for example, Stockmann 1996a, pp. 206-209).

As in other organizations, the methods used by the GTZ to collect and evaluate data for the processing of the check lists have not been systematized, but are left to the consultants themselves. As their stay in the project region is usually short and as the project is very much the centre of interest, they base their evaluation mainly on internal information. It is therefore virtually inevitable that there should be a gap between the theory and practice of PPRs, and although many questions are asked in the guide, the answers to most are unsatisfactory because of the limited insights gained.

In addition to the instruments that have been described above, the GTZ carries out cross-section analyses of the effectiveness of the projects it supports (e.g. 1994 and 1996). The findings are based on interviews with those responsible for projects, which are appraised by external consultants. In terms of methodological approach these cross-section analyses consequently have no new aspects to offer (GTZ 1996a).

As regards methodological questions the GTZ is currently engaged in detailed discussions on the development of its evaluations. To this end it has formed an internal "impact evaluation" team in the staff unit for questions of principle. It is agreed that impact observation should be stepped up and improved in the future. All planning and evaluation tools are currently being reviewed with this end in mind (GTZ 1996).

3.2.4   Evaluation by the German Development Service

One of the foundation stones of the work of the German Development Service (DED), most non-governmental organizations and especially the Church organizations is the idea that the partner is autonomous. Accordingly, the project partners also take responsibility for the planning and implementation and for the evaluation of projects in these organizations. From the goal pursued by the DED and most NGOs of assisting projects that are particularly close to target groups it might be inferred that their evaluation of the social dimension is based on many years of experience. This is true, however, of neither the DED nor the other organizations.

The DED's "first corporate purpose" is the secondment of personnel to partner countries. Only recently has it been realized that the aim cannot be the assignment of a development worker as such, but that the primary concern is the result achieved through the development worker's activities. Accordingly, the DED's established procedures for reviewing projects mainly cover planning elements and take no more than a passing interest in the question of impacts.[11]

The DED's system of **self-evaluation**, which has existed in its present form since 1984, essentially consists of annual reports by the develop- ment workers (monitoring) and an annual review by the country repre- sentative or an expert appointed by him. The **development workers' reports** are guided by their work plans and are target-performance comparisons,[12] on the basis of which the work plans can be updated. The country representatives' **annual reviews**, on the other hand, are based on the programming, which is supplemented by programme progress reports at yearly intervals. If the review findings depart significantly from the programming, fact-finding missions are undertaken or short-term advisers are dispatched from the central office. On the basis of the additional information obtained on the spot, changes are made, if necessary, to the project implementation or to the objectives.

Of late the annual reviews have been made principally by **coordinators** appointed on a sectoral basis and backed up by **regional assistants (RAs)**. Both positions have been newly created at the DED and are intended to perform mediation functions and to improve the staff's knowledge and the organization's backstopping. They will also undertake and reinforce impact observation in the future. The RAs will be drawing up a further annual RA report for this purpose (DED 1997 and 1998a).

On a development worker's return he is usually interviewed at length. However, the discussion is usually restricted to his personal experience,[13] and the specialized experience and know-how he has acquired are not systematically transferred to the institutional memory. Each development worker will therefore be required in the future to complete a questionnaire providing information on project conception, implementation, goal achievement and sustainability when his contract period comes to an end. The results of this exercise will enable a cross-section evaluation to be made and improve the institutional learning process.

Only 0.14 % of the total DED budget is available for overarching **exter- nal evaluations**. Consequently, this tool can be used only for specific purposes, as in cases where significant doubts arise about a project having so far achieved its objectives. Outside evaluators are sometimes supplemented by former development workers if they do not have a formal employment relationship with the DED. A distinction is made between **sectoral and overall evaluations**. An average of one overall evaluation is carried out each year, the organization's whole programme in a host country being examined. As the results of external and self-evaluations largely match, the DED does not see any problem in the clear dominance of self-evaluation in the organization.

The DED's **"second corporate purpose"** is to assist domestic organizations and experts. For this 5 % of the budget is set aside, although the proportion is rising. Only two impact analyses have so far been undertaken in this area, but they were comprehensive.

The DED intends not only to ensure that **impact reviews** are undertaken in the future by making the changes in staff structure mentioned above but also to improve their substance. In all project review tools greater account is to be taken in the future of the impact component. However, the funds available are so limited that the organization's evaluation system cannot be fundamentally modified. The DED therefore undertakes few sustainability studies or social analyses, and the question of impact review methodology is not raised. The organization deliberately refrains from using an evaluation list. Although the staff of the programme department have been calling for the establishment of a system of indicators for some time, it has failed to materialize, again because of the lack of funds. The **partner's involvement** in evaluations is taken for granted at the DED, and interviewing partners is essentially one of the instruments used, but the DED has no instrument of its own with which the partner's view can be systematically recorded in the review reports (see, for example, DED 1998b).

3.2.5   Evaluation by the Church Organizations

The **Church organizations** differ from the DED in their reasons for exercising restraint in impact review. Until the 1980s they tended to be critical of evaluation on principle. Firstly, they criticized the economically and technically dominated approach adopted by the governmental organizations, and secondly, they were convinced that an evaluation initiated unilaterally was inconsistent with the idea of a partnership. As late as 1986 the *Evangelical Centre for Development Aid* (EZE) claimed in a position paper:

> *"Evaluation projects that primarily serve the relief organizations' interest in exercising control and obtaining information and have no more than an indirect impact on the partner organization's work are inconsistent with the principle of partners taking responsibility and the idea of partnership."* (Dütting et al. 1992, pp. 19 f.)

In the meantime, however, the Church organizations too have become convinced of the need for impact observation. This change of mind is put down to the partner's right to find out about the effectiveness of operations. Accordingly, the focus is still on his interest.[14]

On the other hand, the Churches continue to take a critical view of attempts to improve efficiency in development cooperation. Misereor staff comment (Dolzer et al. 1998, pp. 100 f.): *"... solidarity motivated by Christian doctrine often rejects a calculation based on the principle of aid being used as effectively as possible. (...) the quality of action taken in solidarity may suffer if it is geared to the greatest possible efficiency."* This attitude, which is logically derived from Christian beliefs and in which the aim is to remove calculation as a motive, does not, however, exclude consideration of efficiency criteria, as the authors subsequently emphasize: this realization should *"not be used as general absolution from efficiency criteria!"* (Dolzer et al. 1998, pp. 100 f.)

Evaluations are always carried out together with the partner or by him independently, and the "donor organization" plays no more than an advisory and back-up role. If the partner organization lacks experience of conducting evaluations, the "donor organization" also sees it as its task to help the partner to develop procedures for ongoing project monitoring, i.e. to strengthen its evaluation capacities. The aim is to make evaluation an integral part of cooperation and not an endurance test of the partnership, the intention being gradually to overcome the rift in the minds of the "donors" of setting store by clear and critical statements on the one hand and wanting to show consideration for the partners on the other.

The Church organizations' methodological approach does not, however, differ markedly from that of secular organizations. They too undertake target-performance comparisons and means-ends analyses, and they do so as part of a process of reflection and learning conducted with the partner. A development similar to that occurring in governmental organizations is discernible, restricted evaluations that look no further than the project objective having hitherto dominated in Church development cooperation too. Until a few years ago the ToR did not include questions about the effectiveness of operations, the assumption being, as in the other organizations, that the effectiveness of operations *"existed somehow or other"*.

The analytical dimensions of project evaluation are not systematically distinguished from one another in Church development cooperation, and in all projects social issues are the most important aspects of an impact analysis. Evaluations are based on a prescribed reference framework in which the principal questions concern such non-physical criteria as changes in people's awareness, the degree of self-organization and the assertiveness of the target groups. As in other organizations, however, difficulties are again encountered in the formation of indicators.

Given the long and continuing partnerships, it is assumed in Church development cooperation that the timing of project evaluation is not particularly important. At most, a distinction is made between preliminary studies and other evaluations. Evaluations are not carried out to answer questions about continued financing, since the partners are chosen primarily not for the sectors they are in or the problems they have but simply as partners. Once support for certain measures comes to an end, a Church organization normally sets about implementing the next project with the same partner.

The choice of evaluation method in Church cooperation is the partner's responsibility and cannot easily be influenced by the "donors". In its survey and appraisal work Church development cooperation uses methods that have emerged in the environment of participatory approaches to self-help. They are guided primarily by the socio-cultural context and by the specific project conditions.

Methodologically, as the experts involved themselves indicate, a great deal of work still needs to be done to place evaluations on firmer foundations and to systematize them, especially as regards the broader prospect of recording significance and impact. An intensive debate on methodological issues is now in progress, especially at the Evangelical Centre for Development Aid (EZE) and among staff of Misereor. A practical manual on the conception of impacts in development cooperation, with the focus on Church cooperation, appeared in March 1998 (Dolzer et al. 1998).

3.2.6   Evaluation by the Political Foundations

Political foundations such as the Friedrich Ebert Foundation, the Konrad Adenauer Foundation and the Heinrich Böll Foundation also carry out project evaluations. As, however, most types of projects pursue such political objectives as the promotion of democracy and they are therefore no more than indirectly poverty-oriented, projects are not explicitly evaluated for their poverty-reducing effects. Nor is this regarded as a priority.

With the emphasis differing in their work, which is geared to the long term, the political foundations primarily assist organizations which advocate participation in political decision-making processes. They therefore see themselves as political advisers to partner organizations, and their substantive work is geared to changing general conditions through small and specific operations.

The **Konrad Adenauer Foundation (KAS)** is the only political foundation with a long tradition of evaluation and is now able to look back on over 100 project evaluations carried out by external consultants. In 1994 it published a brochure on impact monitoring, which summarizes past experience of evaluations, how they proceeded and what methods were used (Konrad-Adenauer-Stiftung 1994). The foundation's comparative wealth of experience makes a critical appraisal of its past activities possible and enables some weaknesses to be identified. It can be said, for example, that, although the KAS has a well-tried and documented evaluation technique, methodological difficulties occur in almost all its evaluations, particularly because the unclear or very soft objectives formulated during project planning make a target-performance comparison or other evaluations extremely difficult. Nor is it easy, as a rule, to define the target group accurately, which makes it difficult for the consultants to decide on whom the impacts are actually to be reviewed. The KAS has not yet established indicators uniformly with a view to operationalizing impacts. The feedback of evaluation findings into project planning or their local implementation is also considered unsatisfactory within the foundation. These shortcomings and the high cost of evaluations have recently resulted in evaluation being restricted by some of the KAS's departments. Instead, the foundation intends to pay more attention to the methodological problems and to take account of past evaluation findings substantively in order to set learning processes in motion.

The **Friedrich Ebert Foundation (FES)** did not systematize its evaluation activity and develop an evaluation list for the social policy sphere until it redefined its *raison d'être* for the political decision-makers and the public in the early 1990s. Since then rapidly growing importance has been attached to evaluations conducted by external consultants.

When registering the impact of its political work, the foundation considers whether it has in fact had any political influence and whether all opportunities in this respect have been seized. Evaluating influence, on the other hand, is difficult, since no objective statements are possible in the political field. Even in the action taken to achieve major and generally accepted objectives each and every measure is contentious. The FES is currently undertaking a cross-section analysis of past evaluations with the aim of summarizing and assessing the findings and using them specifically to improve its programme work.

Constant quality control, the further development of the programme guidance instruments and conceptual exchanges take precedence in the foundation, however. Evaluations are regarded as part of quality management, quality being maintained by ensuring communication among all the actors with the aid of suitable instruments (reporting, coordination meetings, etc.) and a guidance programme. The guidance programme is based on country concepts which set out the overall goals and on "course sheets", which contain a goal-oriented plan similar to objectives-oriented project planning (ZOPP), including a number of indicators for reviewing the success of the project. The problem here, however, is that the implementation of the measure itself is often shown as an indicator. An evaluation using such indicators can thus be, at best, a performance analysis, not an impact analysis.

In its evaluations the FES acts in accordance with qualitative criteria, since quantitative surveys are considered unjustifiable because of the high cost involved. However, self-evaluation by its partners, who ultimately take responsibility for the outcome of the work, is also considered as important by the FES. This basic conviction does not mean, on the other hand, that the foundation intends to withdraw its commitment to ongoing quality control (Adam 1998, p. 2).

The **Heinrich Böll Foundation (HBS)** has only recently systematized evaluations, developing evaluation guidelines in 1998 (Meentzen 1998, pp. 35 f.). There are plans to have all projects assisted by the HBS evaluated flexibly by external consultants in the form of self-evaluations by the partner organization after half the project period, i.e. after about three years. In substance, the evaluations are principally designed to determine the progress being made towards the achievement of the main project objectives – the promotion of women's interests, gender democracy and the promotion of democracy generally. To this end, terms of reference with appropriate questionnaires were drawn up in May 1998 in close cooperation with the consultants.

The foundation will also be undertaking impact analyses in the future, but only in specific instances because of the high cost involved. They will focus mainly on the impacts of advanced training schemes, public relations work through alternative media and gender issues. A problem that has yet to be solved is the establishment of criteria for the operationalization of impacts.

Questions about the inquiry method to be used in evaluations and impact analyses have not yet been explicitly raised in the HBS. Instead, the approach adopted and the manner in which data are collected largely depend on the consultants or the partner organizations, a decision being taken as a function of the project, theme, budget and assessment team. On the whole, preference is given to deciding on a case-by-case basis without any overly rigid prescriptions.

3.3   Conclusions, or Ten Evaluation Problems

As the description of evaluation in German development cooperation shows, the type of evaluation preferred by each organization depends on its particular function in the field of development policy and is also closely linked to its tradition and the types of project it mainly assists. This explains, for example, why ex post analyses are of greater interest to the BMZ for strategic reasons and to financial cooperation for reasons associated with the specific project, whereas ex ante reviews and evaluations during project implementation are of primary interest in the case of technical cooperation. While financial cooperation projects come to a clearly definable end, the conventional project cycle in technical cooperation is being increasingly called into question by the ongoing nature of the cooperation. While evaluations for the BMZ, KfW and organizations that do not have long-term experts working for them locally are carried out mainly by external consultants, the GTZ and non-governmental organizations clearly prefer self-evaluations, since they tend to accelerate institutional learning and are less costly.

Despite the convergence of governmental and non-governmental organizations' views on what constitutes evaluation, they continue to differ on quality and efficiency and the involvement of partners. While the Churches emphasize the idea of solidarity and so shun excessive concentration of efficiency for its own sake, the GTZ emphasizes a concept of quality that focuses on the client, i.e. the partner and target group. Budgets also differ. The large organizations are able to consider methodological issues in depth, while the small ones have no choice but to learn from the others' experience.

It can also be said that the social dimension is seen in very different terms by the various organizations. While the socio-cultural aspects are emphasized in financial cooperation, with the focus squarely on the acceptance and legitimacy aspects, greater emphasis is placed on participation in the case of technical cooperation and the non-governmental organizations. Systematic impact observation in which account is taken of the distribution of the benefits of a project is still uncharted territory for most development organizations. As the few observations of impacts hitherto undertaken have, moreover, been very closely guided by the project objectives, little or no account has been taken of unintended effects. Few primary surveys of the changing lives of the target groups have been purposefully included in the past, or data on this aspect frequently has taken the form of forecasts or been based on information whose source lacks transparency.

All current ideas on how to record project impacts are inadequate. Most concepts consist of a more or less haphazard stringing together of conventional or participatory inquiry methods. Equally, there are no basic concepts for the operationalization of poverty reduction, "optimum participation" or targeted benefits of a project. Instead, it is usually left to the evaluation teams to decide how impact observations should proceed and what methods to use, and they often have no time to consider methodological questions in any depth.

Although questions about the social dimension are increasingly raised in the evaluation lists of the BMZ and certain organizations, the result so far has merely been to lengthen the lists of questions, with nothing done to clarify methodological issues. Accordingly, the validity and reliability of evaluation findings and the methods applied have seldom been questioned in the past. This shortcoming is partly due to the fact that technical thinking long dominated development cooperation and very little importance was attached to social scientists and methodological specialists. The teaching of the methods of the social sciences does not form part of the training of scientists, technicians or economists. These are, however, skills that are needed for the development of a complete evaluation concept.[15]

The ten urgent problems in evaluation as seen by the various organizations themselves, with the emphasis placed on different aspects, are the following:

(1) **The problem of attributing impacts (*attribution gap*)**
(*Crisis of verification*)
The current instruments do not have sufficient range to cover the social dimension and to attribute impacts. The causality problem is further exacerbated when several actors or donors are to be found in a project region and when programmes or projects have long impact chains, as is increasingly the case.

(2) **Deficient operationalization of the targeted benefits of a project**
(*Crisis of accreditation*)
There are currently very few concepts for the operationalization of programme and project impacts (e.g. poverty reduction, capacity-building, democracy). This becomes even more critical in higher level evaluations that get increasingly important. Communication between researchers and practitioners is neither sufficient nor fruitful.

(3) **Lack of transparency in terms of the evaluation method**
The majority of evaluations are undertaken without any explicit methodological concept, and the majority of evaluation reports do not include a sufficiently differentiated section on methods. The approach adopted in evaluations consequently continues to lack transparency.

(4) **Lack of comparability of evaluation reports**
The lack of standardization and comparability of evaluation reports has a particularly adverse effect in cross-section analyses.

(5) **Time-consuming and costly nature of evaluations compared to project budgets**
Financial constraints now impose strict limits on evaluation by all organizations, but the room for manoeuvre is particularly tight in the case of micro-projects and NGOs.

(6) **Problem of vested interests and the counterpart's fears, inadequate involvement of the partner in evaluations**
At present evaluations are rarely initiated by the partner. Where a de-

cision is to be taken on continued financing, the partner's openness is extremely limited. It is still common for the target group not to be regarded as an equal partner in the team. But also joint evaluations of different donors are difficult to initiate.

(7) **Shortcomings in the formulation of the objectives of the project**

As NGOs sometimes fail to use systematic planning instruments in their project planning, objectives are not formulated accurately, thus sometimes depriving project-related evaluations of a proper basis.

(8) **Inadequate systematization of indicators and the weighting of indicators**

Criteria and lists of indicators have frequently been drawn up, but the choice of indicators is often regarded as unsatisfactory, as when the implementation of a measure is itself used as an indicator. The problem of the weighting of several indicators for the description of a phenomenon has yet to be solved by any organization. As new indicators are constantly being chosen, the problem of the limited comparability of the results persists.

(9) **Unclarified handling of the time-lag and the limited period over which impacts occur**

Project impacts and especially social changes often occur with a pronounced time-lag. How this time-lag is determined and handled has yet to be clarified. The same applies to the period over which impacts occur. This is a particularly serious evaluation problem in ex post analyses.

(10) **Inadequate feedback and follow-up of evaluation findings (*Crisis of utilization*)**

Although the utilization of evaluation findings in subsequent planning has been systematized in the large governmental organizations, actual learning steps frequently lag behind what was originally intended even in such organizations. On the whole, institutional learning from evaluation findings is still inadequate.

On balance it can be said that, although there are still many shortcomings in evaluation today, they have been recognized by the majority of institutions.[16] The problems referred to and the many discussions currently taking place on this subject in the policy field are an indication of the urgent need for the development of methods. All the institutions are agreed that greater emphasis must be placed on impact analysis with the focus on the social dimension. Their views differ on whether this should be done within the framework of existing planning and evaluation tools or of new tools. Integration into the existing range of tools is conceivable in all the large organizations, whereas the smaller ones have yet to develop this range, or they are able to use analyses more flexibly and are not dependent on standardization in the same way.

One reason for the slow progress of institutional learning despite the recognition of the shortcomings is the very limited exchange of information between researchers and practitioners[17] and the inadequate international orientation of communication. The latter gives rise to coordination problems that pose major difficulties particularly when several donor organizations from different countries are operating in the same region, as is increasingly the case.

Nor have many signals yet been given by the politicians. The evaluation goals formulated by the political parties in a motion jointly tabled by all the political groups in the Bundestag on 28 May 1998 do, however, include these signals:

> "To be effective, evaluations must be as systematic and objective, as closely related to the situation and culture as possible, impartial and independent, methodologically appropriate, credible and, above all, policy-oriented for the decision-makers. In accordance with the principles of partnership and participation, all parties involved in the development project concerned should also in principle take part in the evaluation process."

To clarify the significance of these requirements, which the politicians believe "good evaluation practice" should satisfy, and to analyse it, a number of theoretical aspects of evaluation research and various evaluation concepts first need to be considered in greater depth. Before practical methods are selected or developed, it will also be helpful to gain a rough impression of the pros and cons of various survey and assessment methods in empirical social research. To this end, methodological questions of a more general nature are also considered in the fourth chapter. Then, in the fifth chapter, a method of analysing the social impacts of target-group-oriented types of project is devised and tested empirically. An attempt is made in this context to come closer to satisfying the requirements of evaluations that have been formulated and to take account of at least some of the ten problem areas listed above.

4   Evaluation Concepts and Methods

4.1   Conventional Evaluation Designs

Impact analyses are based on the assumption that project operations trigger effects in the counterpart organization, target groups and project environment. It is assumed that there is a causal link between project activities and impacts and that measurable effects occur by means of direct or indirect diffusion processes (Stockmann 1996b, pp. 80 ff.). This simplistic idea of cause-and-effect links forms the basis of the analytical approach in impact analysis and is not questioned here, even though more complex models that take account of correlations or synergies might be taken as a basis.

Scientifically, the impact of project operations can be measured only if it is known what the situation would have been if the operation had not taken place.[1] It has to be demonstrated that a change in the dependent variables (project impact) is due to the independent variables (project operation). Accordingly, a distinction is made between the gross and net impacts of an operation. In theory, the net impact of an intervention can be determined by isolating the disturbance variables, a distinction being made between endogenous disturbance variables, which are due to the design of the evaluation, and exogenous disturbance factors, such as environmental effects extraneous to the operation.

This basis of scientific research faces the social sciences with insurmountable difficulties, since disturbance variables can be isolated only in "social laboratory experiments", which are in fact hardly feasible and often of questionable benefit. If something closer to ideal impact analysis is to be achieved, comparison is therefore the most important element in evaluation research. It may consist in comparing different groups (cross-section or counterfactual approach) or situations at different times (longitudinal section). What is important is that the situations with and without the operation are compared so that comprehensible findings may be produced.

Experimental designs and quasi-experimental designs are based on the comparison of a test group and a control group (with-and-without comparison). The test group is exposed to the planned operation, the control group is not. While a "genuine" randomized control is used in an experimental design, a control group equivalent to the test group in respect of the most important variables is constructed in a quasi-experimental design.[2]

It is assumed in this approach that the net effect can be determined by comparing the gross effects on the two groups. The basis of the experimental design is therefore:

Net impact = gross impact on the test group – gross impact on the control group

This study design presupposes that the test and control groups are qualitatively comparable before the operation and were exposed to the same general influences. It must be ensured that the operation would have had the same impact on the control group as on the test group. In reality this is rarely the case, since the external influences in a region, for example, are usually very heterogeneous.

A possible solution to a problem situation of this kind might be to use sufficiently large a number of cases to achieve the desired comparability by means of significance tests. This, however, is one of the general problems of evaluation research, since it operates with a study topic – projects – with which there are, as a rule, few comparable cases, each having very many variables. It is therefore seldom possible to evaluate sufficiently large random samples for a comparison to be statistically valid.

Leaving aside the comparability problems, even though, in the final analysis, they basically question the experimental approach to evaluations, only this design corresponds to the ideal of a rigorous impact analysis. If external disturbance factors are isolated from the study, impact links can be recorded with an accuracy that is not otherwise to be achieved in the social sciences. Through the use of rigid causal analyses a high degree of internal validity and reliability can be attained. They alone are likely to prove causality assumptions.[3]

Besides the comparability problem, however, experimental research design poses further problems as regards practical feasibility, since it is very expensive and time-consuming and not very sensitive to minor changes. Creating control groups is also difficult, both when evaluation is carried out at a high level of aggregation and a control group consists of a whole country and when it takes place at project level. In the latter case the "control group" would consist, for example, of a village community, which would be expected to undergo lengthy appraisals for research purposes without itself being able to benefit from them in any way. An evaluation design of this kind casts the target group in a purely passive role ("extractive research"), which contrasts with the present approach, where the partner or target group is intended to play an active part in all project decisions.

Unlike experimental designs, non-experimental designs make for a lesser degree of internal validity, but they are quicker and cheaper to implement and do not harm the integrity of the target groups in the same way. To determine the impact of project activities, the with-and-without comparison gives way to a time comparison, i.e. a before-and-after comparison. The term "non-experimental design" is not, however, based on a fixed concept, but is used as a collective term for all forms of non-experimental impact analysis. Reflexive reviews form the most stringent of the non-experimental designs: the test group forms its own control group by comparing measurements of the study unit observed before the operation with subsequent measurements. The assumption underlying these designs is:

> Net impact = gross impact after the operation – gross impact before the operation

The validity of reflexive monitoring is based on the assumption that external effects remain constant during the study period. In real projects, however, this is never the case, since a project continues for several years, during which the environment always changes in some way. Consequently, major uncertainties are always attached to the outcome of a comparison of this kind. A further difficulty is that the number of cases is not as a rule sufficiently high for the results to be statistically safe. Another problem frequently encountered in practice is the absence of a prior analysis of a project that is to undergo an impact analysis. This often makes it impossible for an evaluator to carry out a before-and-after analysis.

The most frequent approach in evaluation is therefore to carry out shadow and generic reviews. However, these tools lie in the grey area of scientific analytical techniques. They are based on experts' personal or collective judgements. From their experience and the secondary information available to them they estimate what would have happened if the operation had not taken place. In generic checks evaluators use secured measurement parameters rather than a control group as the basis for comparison, i.e. they make a comparison with facts that are accepted as being "normal". The dependence on vague checks of this kind is the main reason for its still being so important in evaluation who carries out a study, since the evaluator's experience, intuition and skills are virtually the only means of assessing validity and reliability.

4.2   The Change in the Conception of Evaluation

The discussion of the various approaches from a theoretical angle shows why the resulting evaluation reports are afflicted with the problems of poor intersubjective verifiability and poor transparency to which reference was made in the previous section.

As early as 1984 Legge referred to a threefold crisis in evaluation research. Findings are not utilized (crisis of utilization), their validity and significance are often questionable (crisis of verification), and the value judgments that find their way into the research are not well thought out and barely explained (crisis of accreditation).[4] In the late 1970s this unsatisfactory situation led to the development of qualitative concepts on the basis of other theoretical concepts that include ethnographic approaches.

Patton (1978), for example, emphasized the need for utilization-focused evaluation and attempted in particular to find an answer to the problem that existed even then of the inadequate utilization of evaluation findings. The primary objective should be not methodological purity, but the political relevance and usability of the findings for decision-makers. He deliberately eschewed the goal of scientific objectivity, replacing it with the criterion of "fairness".[5] A few years later Bryk (1983) was one of the first researchers to call not only for project evaluations to be left to external consultants but also for everyone participating in the project, including the target groups, to be involved in the study as evaluators (stakeholder approach) (Bryk 1983). He thus placed the emphasis on the process of identifying the actual users of evaluation findings, while qualifying the idea that only one reality is valid for everyone.

Guba and Lincoln (1987) (quoted from Guba / Lincoln 1989) in particular took up what were at that time new ideas and stimulated further debate. In their naturalistic evaluation approach in fourth-generation evaluation they defined earlier evaluation approaches as measurement, description and, finally, appropriate assessment, whereas in the fourth generation they equated evaluation with a process of negotiation among all concerned.

Guba / Lincoln (1989, pp. 252 ff.) see evaluation as a socio-political process which includes the political and cultural elements that encompass all human activities. According to their ideas, it would not therefore be appropriate to attempt to "eliminate" the political and cultural elements by using "artificial" (e.g. experimental and quantitative) methods; they should in fact be integrated and themselves become part of the study.

The authors see an evaluation as a continuous process of cooperation and joint learning in which outcomes are created rather than found. In their opinion, the actors need not necessarily agree on these outcomes: even disagreement can be identified as an outcome of evaluation. In evaluations seen in these terms the aim is not to find an objective truth: truth is rather the construction of a well informed and, if possible, differentiated idea at a given time, and it is also renewable or modifiable at any time.

This constructivist view might give the impression that the created outcomes are somewhat arbitrary. However, even radical constructivists assume that subjective views also concern reality,[6] since one can only mean what reality also anticipates, rather as Olaf Müller would have it: "... *when I talk about owls, I mean owls, what else?"* (Müller 1996). In other words, it is assumed that there is an "objective" world which is independent of consciousness or transphenomenal. This is contrasted by Roth (1994, pp. 288 and 321), for example, with "factuality" (objective reality) rather than "appearance" (perceived reality). The ideas that people have about the composition of reality are therefore useful in arriving at a better explanation of the phenomena of their own reality.

Although an evaluation never ends where a consistently constructivist view is taken, it continues to be concluded with a decision in practice. It does not, however, claim to be the only possible, true decision. Nonetheless, an attempt should be made in an evaluation to take the decision that is valid for as many actors as possible, on the principle that a hypothesis that is valid for both A and B is rejected if it is not valid for A and B together[7] and that, therefore, a joint evaluation that is as closely related to reality as possible is eventually designed.

So open a view of evaluation ideally leads from a narrow, absolute view to a comprehensive, qualifying view. Instead of account being rendered, responsibility is to be shared; instead of data being utilized, empowerment is the goal. The approach hitherto adopted by external evaluators, described by Guba / Lincoln as *"ignorant and problem-oriented"*, would give way to understanding and respect for all actors. Instead of demobilizing, evaluation would then stimulate action.

Despite these approaches, which already belong to the past, the gap between the goal and reality in evaluation has not been closed in the intervening period of almost ten years. Although the findings of quantitatively oriented studies regularly cause disappointment and all those commissioning evaluations are equally aware of the poor scientific quality of many qualitative evaluations conducted without a methodological conception, fundamental and conscious reorientation has yet to occur and the "face validity" of quantitative studies has yet to be disproved. The greatest difficulties in this context consist in abandoning or qualifying the following view, which stems from a positivist attitude:

— **Accepting multiple realities as a basis for decisions**
    How are unambiguous decisions to be taken where there are different perceptions of reality?

    Answer: The decisions are negotiated; there is no one true decision, only created outcomes of negotiation.

— **Subjectivity of the studies, limited validity and therefore an increased need for external legitimation**
    What checks can be made on qualitative studies? How is their validity to be rated?

    Answer: Such techniques as triangulation (information is verified with the help of a second source) and context validation (the reliability of the informant is verified by triangulation) can be used. During auditing the correctness of the research findings can also be verified by an expert auditor in accordance with a specified set of rules.

— **Limited generalizability**
    What informative value can be deduced from the high degree of specificity of qualitative appraisals?

    Answer: Generalizability is not a primary objective of evaluation research; nor can it be justified in the theory of science. Instead, it is linked to the practice of many different forms of advice on organization, which is very closely related to the individual case.

— **Danger of "going native" (the researcher identifies with the participants)**
    Does intensive interaction result in the researcher's identification with the objects of his research?

Answer: Systematic attempts at monitoring would consist not only in the researcher's own thoughts on interaction (e.g. in the form of a research journal) but also in the observation or debriefing of the researcher, in which he himself becomes the informant and is regularly interviewed by colleagues not involved in the research. Another possibility is to divide the research team or to change its composition constantly.

If the validity criterion is abandoned and the constructivist, hermeneutic and pragmatic conceptions of the social sciences are adopted, the emphasis shifts to the criterion of dialogue. The truth is arrived at during the dialogue, and claims to validity arise, according to Salner (1986) (quoted from Kalve 1991, p. 429), in the medium of conflicting interpretations, which are communicated between and negotiated by the people participating in the activities and decision-making. Communicative validation includes the discursive verification of the validity of claims to knowledge. Habermas bases communicative validation on the consensus theory, i.e. the discourse is ideally geared to universally valid truths. The coherence and internal consistency of the line of argument become extremely important. A form of validity of this kind cannot be equated with an "intersubjective reality", which occurs, for example, where a large number of independent concurring observations are available. This would be simplistic and mere consensualism. Consensus is instead regarded only as an intermediate stage at which new ideas, differentiations and rules on the discourse are generated.

In the social sciences various concepts of communicative validation are to be found primarily in psychoanalysis and systems evaluation. House (1980) has pointed out that the main task of evaluation research should be to indicate new lines of communication to the readers of a research report and to find answers to new questions. The methodology presented in the fifth chapter should also be viewed from this angle.

Given the many methodologically unsatisfactory evaluation reports in the past that maintained the claim to conventional validity without coming anywhere near to achieving it, it is easy to see why the approaches to qualitative validation that have been described are favourably received in practice where they are adopted. A view that is offensively advanced in the GTZ today, for example, is that it is appropriate to drop the claim to proof of causality. Instead, it should be accepted that the attribution of impacts in evaluations is only ever based on plausibility (Kuby 1997a, p. 11; Kuby 1997b, p. 12; GTZ 1998b, p. 22.). Rather than vainly searching for evidence, the aim should be to keep the attribution gap as narrow as possible by seeking, for example, to increase plausibility through the introduction of new methodological elements. This approach is discussed at greater length in the next section and forms part of the foundations in the empirical part of this study.

4.3   The Impact Model of the GTZ's Internal Evaluation Team

In its impact model the GTZ's Internal Evaluation Team breaks down the various levels of observation or data areas in evaluations and describes their respective ranges (Figure 4).[8]

In practical evaluations today a project-related approach is usually adopted, the outputs and outcomes of projects being evaluated on the basis of the inputs. While the inputs can be derived from the project documents and are therefore easy to evaluate, determining the outputs and outcomes is often very difficult and possibly very costly (see the explanations in Chapter 5). Even then, however, the range of this approach to determining impacts is too small for statements to be possible.

In evaluations that seek to be comprehensive and in impact evaluations it therefore seems appropriate to include a further perspective and to be guided not only by the project but also by the reality of the lives of the people or target groups. This reality is symbolized by the oval in the upper right-hand corner of the impact model shown in Figure 4. Where such basic data are available and the change in them during the project cycle is observed, the causes of the change can then be attributed to project activities or ascribed to external factors. However, this means that the attribution gap persists regardless of whether the approach adopted is project-related or context-related. On the other hand, the gap narrows significantly when the evaluation is made from both sides, i.e. it is both project- and context-related. Where information is available from all data

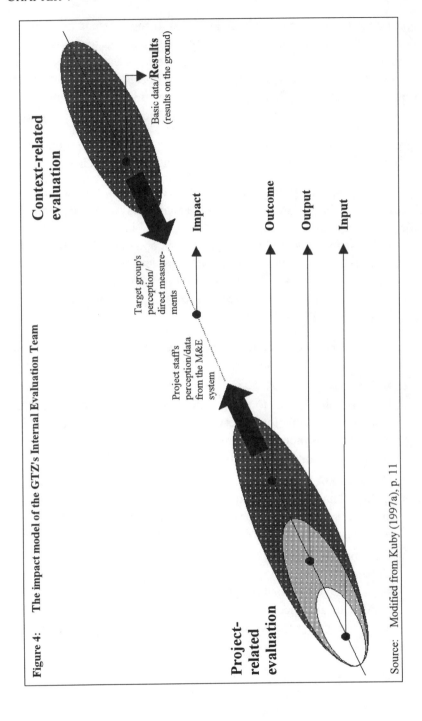

Figure 4: The impact model of the GTZ's Internal Evaluation Team

Source: Modified from Kuby (1997a), p. 11

areas, the effect or impact can be localized to some extent, as shown in the model. The remaining bridgehead should, in the team's view, be achieved through a comparison of project outcomes and the results on the ground. Where more than one organization is operating at the locality, the separate attribution of impacts by the various donors and a subsequent comparison of the assessments can be used to increase plausibility further.

The model presented is used below, since it shows the various data areas for evaluations and their ranges separately and in a comprehensible form.

For a better understanding and to explain the model, the various data areas that have to be covered by an impact analysis are first illustrated in the following with the help of examples: the oval in the bottom left-hand corner of the model symbolizes input, output and outcome data. Ideally, such data are included in a project's M&E system. They comprise information on costs and project activities and on technical achievements and their direct benefits. These project-related data enable project goal achievement to be reviewed.

The various data areas are defined here as they are understood in the OED:

— **Input data**
    Input variables relate to the quantity (and sometimes quality) of the resources available for project activities (e.g. funds, guarantees, human resources, number of person-months, cost of advanced training, equipment / material / supplies).

— **Output data**
    Output data indicate the quantity (and sometimes quality) of the goods or services which have been created through the use of the inputs (e.g. people vaccinated, kilometres of road built, trees planted).

— **Outcome and impact data**
    Outcome and impact data measure the quantity and quality of the results achieved with the project goods and services (e.g. reduced number of sick people, improved sustainability of farming). (But there is a difference of outcome and impact data explained as follows.)

Taking a resource protection project as an example, input data represent, say, the number of seedlings sold, the number of donkey carts subsidized or the number of shovels distributed. The output would then be the number of seedlings planted and the length of contour ridges built with stones that have been transported with the help of the donkey carts. In the third case a conceivable output would be the extent to which a natural water cistern has been enlarged with the help of the shovels distributed by the project. For the last two cases, however, many other uses beside that planned are possible. Outcome data overlap impact data, since they already include information on the benefit of an activity. However, while outcome data describe the direct benefit which can also be a *means* to reach further goals (*ends*), the impact data show the effect deduced from the sum of the outcomes, i.e. *ends* that derived from reaching several *means*. The impact data also include unintended effects (see Figure 4). In the examples chosen the outcome of an operation would be the quantity of tree crops harvested or the increase in yield achieved through the reclamation of fertile land. In the third case the determining factor would be the increase in the number of days or weeks that the cistern remained full before drying up and was used to water domestic animals.

Depending on the nature of the project activity, the collection of output and outcome data may, as these comments already indicate, be very time-consuming and difficult,[9] and even then the data are sometimes inadequate for practical use.[10] These difficulties are also among the reasons for output and outcome data rarely being measured. Measuring all project results would not be at all appropriate on cost grounds. It is far more appropriate to limit the collection of such data to operations whose potential benefit is doubtful. Some measurements can, moreover, be replaced with less time-consuming qualitative observations. It should first be considered, for example, whether a survey of the target group would not produce sufficient information. Thus farmers undoubtedly have no problem providing qualitative data on the impacts on yields which they have seen resource protection facilities have on their millet fields.

The data area symbolized by the oval in the upper right-hand corner of the impact model represents the "basic data" or "results on the ground" that provide information on the actual lives of the people in a project region.

Only with the help of these data is it possible to identify social changes, which for the purposes of an impact analysis have to be reviewed to see if they are due to project activities or to external factors. The point marked "impact" on the broken line in the model indicates the social changes triggered by project activities. However, as social changes are as a rule caused by a range of factors rather than factors that can be isolated from one another and as the environmental situation also plays a part in this context, this point is located precisely half way between the directly measurable data areas depicted.[11]

To illustrate this, the examples of project activities chosen above will again be taken to show the likely social effects of the operations. In the case of fruit tree plantations the impact would manifest itself in an improved nutritional status as a result of a diet with a higher vitamin content or in easier access to firewood. The target group might, however, use the timber to roof their huts. In the case of the donkey carts the impact could be described as the improved health of the people owing to the increase in agricultural productivity brought about by the stone lines and the resulting improvement in the nutritional status of the people. The donkey carts might, however, be used primarily to carry sick people and so account for the improvement in health status. In the case of the en-larged cistern the impact might again manifest itself in an improved nutritional status due to better animal husbandry and utilization of animal products. However, the improvement in nutrition could also be due to the growing of more vegetables because of the increased availability of water.

The examples make it clear that impact analysis very soon resorts to speculation if it is based on the project operations. Unplanned impacts cannot be discerned in this way, nor can the parts played by individual operations in an impact be identified. It is less time-consuming to deduce project impacts from the changes in people's lives and so to undertake a context-related analysis. Unintended impacts are then covered in exactly the same way as intended impacts, and a monocausal view of the relation-ship between operation and effect, which hardly exists in reality, can be replaced with the multiple-factor explanation of impacts. The design of the evaluation in the empirical part of this study is based on this approach.

Before this is discussed, current survey and appraisal methods should be considered and those selected that seem suitable for context-related impact analysis.

4.4   From Conventional to Participatory Evaluation

With the growing importance of orientation towards the target group and self-help approaches in development cooperation in the 1980s, participatory survey methods gained in importance almost as a complement to participation in cost-sharing and participation in decision-making. The greater need for project evaluations was generally recognized at about the same time. The combination of the two elements to form "participatory evaluation (PE)" did not occur until a few years later, however, and follows on logically from the evolution of the image of evaluation, which has been described above.

Participatory evaluation is based on a stakeholder approach, the underlying principle being that *"people on the receiving end are ultimately the best judges of impact whether benefits have been produced or not"* (Kamla 1985). Participatory instruments are meant to close the social and cognitive gap between domestic and foreign project staff on the one hand and the target group on the other. The assumption here is that this method makes development results more accessible and the evaluation process becomes more specific and more vivid.[12] A participatory approach thus provides an opportunity for evaluations to be made more effective and more efficient. As evaluations conducted in this way also increase the target group's identification with the project, ownership is also promoted. This in turn makes it more likely that the project will be sustainable and have a wide impact.

A further argument for participatory evaluations lies in the principle on which the participatory approach is based. According to Schneider / Libercier (1995, p. 39), participation means

"a partnership built upon the basis of a dialogue among the various actors (stakeholders), during which the agenda is set jointly, and local views and indigenous knowledge are deliber-

ately sought and respected. This implies negotiation rather than the dominance of an externally set agenda. Thus people become actors instead of being simply beneficiaries (...)."

In line with this conviction the process of participatory evaluation is an element in strengthening the self-confidence of the target group and achieving its active involvement in the whole development process in contrast to the role played by the passive beneficiary.[13] Participatory evaluation therefore has a further important opportunity of making all concerned realize that the target group not only has labour resources available but is also capable of contributing ideas, talents and creativity as well as accountability and management skills.

In recent years participatory evaluation has been generally approved in development organizations.[14] In the Bundestag too all parties now recognize that the participation of the target groups throughout the project cycle, which includes evaluations, is decisive for the success or failure of development cooperation (Schuster / Pinger 1998, p. 160).

Participatory evaluation also conforms to the approach of the client-oriented quality concept, in which feedback from the client on the quality of the product is of prime importance for quality management.[15] This tendency in technical cooperation also makes it almost impossible today to disparage participatory evaluations as being '"too subjective".

Within the research community, however, the participatory approach is still viewed with pronounced scepticism in some quarters, since allowing the "object" of research to become the "researcher" is inconsistent with the conventional principles of the social sciences which have already been discussed. The assumption is that the target group's participation in the evaluation process threatens the validity of the evaluation findings; the target group's participation should consist solely in the provision of information, not in the evaluation of data.[16]

What the proponents of this position usually overlook, however, is that ignoring the partner's view is also bound to lead to distorted results, since even the conventional approach to evaluation comprises the analysis of findings that are "perceived", not of objectively measurable data. The qualitative analysis of data obtained by non-experimental methods is influenced by subjectivity in the same way as the analysis of data obtained from participatory surveys.

The constructivist approach is based on the pluralism of values, i.e. there is no objectively verified reality: reality is always a construct reflecting a given perspective (for further comments see sections 3.1.2 and 4.2). From this angle all views may contribute to the finding of reality, even if each is influenced by different interests or describes only a section of reality. Subjectivity is not seen as an obstacle to finding reality, but the inclusion of all fundamental subjective assessments leads to a reality that is valid for everyone. Where possible, direct measurements can, however, complement subjective views along the lines of triangulation.

A further argument against the criticism emanating from the research community is that there is a lack of alternatives to the participatory approach. Evaluations based on the usual set of instruments and carried out with the aid of semi-structured interviews of individuals have already proved to have little validity in many cases. Basing evaluations on large-scale, quantitative surveys or on experimental designs, on the other hand, is very time-consuming and also gives rise to fundamental problems, which have already been discussed. The participatory approach presents itself, as it were, as a methodological way out, even though it is not a fundamentally better solution as regards the validity of the results.

There are also a few other risks inherent in the participatory approach. Unless the concept is filled with the specific substance of the various countries and cultures, there is a danger of the western approach to participation being imposed. Where participatory approaches encounter societies with a strict hierarchical structure, the participants may find it incompatible with their way of thinking and their system of values. In such cases too, critics of participatory evaluation therefore describe the approach as "acultural".

A further risk inherent in participatory evaluations is that the participation of domestic organizations or institutions may lead to the revival of certain societal or hierarchical structures or structures influenced by particularist interests, even though they are in no way compatible with the project goals, since they are, for example, inconsistent with the idea of emancipation. Dominant opinion-leaders within an otherwise passive target group may also suggest their perception to the group or impose it on them if the evaluation team does not intervene. On the other hand, participatory procedures may be rejected and prevented by leading elites in the project region if, for example, they are afraid that not enough account will be taken of their interests.

If excessive emphasis is placed on communicative processes in the participatory approach, there is also a danger that the desired orientation towards decision-making will be abandoned for endless communication loops and that no result at all will be produced in the end, despite a considerable investment of time. Such "communication fundamentalism" is not an invention of opponents of participation, as might at first be thought: it actually exists within some projects. One evaluation report states, for example:

> "... Conversations with field advisers sometimes convey the impression that the teams (for organizational capacity building in villages; S.N.) had become 'encounter groups' at that time. (...) More and more dimensions of village society and increasingly profound causes of institutional situations that might be important variables were perceived – in principle, ad infinitum. (...) As regards the development of an operational approach the effects were disastrous: the conceptual prescriptions (...) led to a kind of 'operation minimalism'. (...) Self-observation coupled with the conception of the 'singularity' of the experience gained in each village triggered competitive thinking and particularism among the field teams (...). In some villages the inconsistent approaches, the seemingly aimless chatting of the field teams and the absence of deeds caused astonishment, confusion and fatigue. In some villages the teams' ignorance of relationships within and between villages led to misunderstandings, in some cases to tensions and even to the rekindling of conflicts that had been buried."

An approach of this nature, which leads to the paralysis of a whole project area and may eventually do considerable damage, does not, however, in any way correspond to the original purpose of participatory approaches, but runs counter to it. It stems rather from the conventional ethnological approach, in which there is indeed a tendency for observation and description to be pursued as ends in themselves. For a project management team such an approach is a paradox from the outset, since operation minimalism, like excessive actionism, is bound to result in a project failing. The art consists in striking a balance between communication and coordination on the one hand and decision-making, implementation and, again, reflection on what has been done, on the other hand. Striking this balance in projects is often difficult. The various approaches are frequently adopted by the project staff according to their affiliation to various professional groups (typically, technicians versus social scientists), which encourages polarization. There is thus a danger of the only chance of a project succeeding, which consists in combining these soft skills with the hard skills, being gambled away.

It is a fact, of course, that participatory approaches and evaluations, and all processes based on coordination, take more time than would be needed for an assessment or decision arrived at hierarchically or by one side. The longer it takes, the more it costs initially, although the prospects for sustainability and general acceptance also improve. The World Bank, however, has estimated that participatory evaluations cost only 10 - 15 % more than conventional evaluations (Schneider / Libercier 1995, p. 58).

The International Fund for Agricultural Development/IFAD (IFAD 1992) believes that the greatest problem with participatory evaluations hitherto carried out lies at a completely different level. It sees the most serious difficulties being posed by the in some respects limited implementation of evaluation results obtained through participation. A number of very promising evaluations have failed, it claims, because the results obtained and plans drawn up jointly had not been implemented, leading to frustration and withdrawal on the part of the target group. There is no point in obtaining evaluation results if they are not going to be taken seriously. If there are no means of implementing them, it is preferable to forgo the pretence of participation (Uphoff 1985, p. 381).

4.5   From Quantitative to Qualitative Methods

In principle, quantitative or qualitative methods can be used to collect and analyse data for evaluations. In empirical social research these approaches are based on different and in some respects opposite scientific paradigms, which are also reflected in the evaluation designs.

In many cases, however, quantitative and qualitative methods can be combined, thus enabling their respective advantages to be exploited and their respective disadvantages to be offset. The choice of method should therefore be guided primarily by its suitability for processing different problems and not by positions in the conflict of opinions.

In a **quantitative approach** the research object is ideally measured as such or with the aid of indicators and related to other measurement data of the same type. Where the data set is sufficiently large and valid, correlations and weightings between variables can then be identified, for example, by means of regression analyses. In the evaluation of a resource protection development project, for instance, particularly successful project operations might be identified and weighted in terms of their erosion-reducing impact. If the information required is accurate enough and can be measured as it stands and if the question calls for a quantitative answer, an approach of this kind may be the only appropriate one.

The quantitative approach requires sufficiently large sets of data. For project evaluations, however, such quantities of data can be collected only in rare cases within an acceptable period and at a reasonable cost. To determine the influence of external factors and isolate them from the project impacts to be evaluated, a large number of comparable projects in different regions are also needed. As such large numbers do not usually exist, doubts about the reliability of the data often persist. With a smaller, quantitatively oriented data sample based on a few cases, on the other hand, the limits to admissible statistical evaluation procedures are soon encountered. If the statistical operations are nonetheless carried out – as often happens in practice – a degree of accuracy and validity which does not in truth exist is simulated with the results. If, however, no more than percentage statements are made, the results are frequently of limited informational value.

In the case of a subject matter in the field of the social sciences – i.e. in evaluation research too – the clarifying variables frequently defy definition from the outset. If the study is nevertheless to be restricted to the essential and no data graveyards are to be produced – as so easily happens with quantitative methods – relatively clearly limited hypotheses need to be formulated in advance of the study. On the basis of these hypotheses a more or less closed and usually standardized inquiry pattern, which cannot then be modified or adjusted during the study, is normally devised. This deductive approach may result in failure to identify variables that may be important. Jodha (1988; quoted from World Bank, no year) reports in this context of a case study in India in which quantitative surveys of poverty trends in a region revealed sharp drops in per capita income, whereas a participatory, qualitative survey of the same population group showed that many other poverty criteria of equal importance to the people had improved significantly.[17]

Jodha sees the main cause of such shortcomings in the communication gap between the evaluator and the group of respondents, which can result in inappropriate criteria being selected and incorrect yardsticks being adopted. Particularly for surveys in an unfamiliar cultural context there is a high risk of incorrect or irrelevant results being obtained with quantitative methods. Lenz (1992) advances several arguments to back what she sees as the greater suitability of qualitative approaches, especially for research in developing countries: firstly, as developing countries often lack basic data in the form of reliable administrative and vital statistics, they have few references for surveys of their own, and because of unfounded expectations or fears strategies of refusal and manipulation adopted by interviewees easily lead to incorrect results, and intercultural differences of meaning of definitional concepts give rise to incorrect conclusions, especially in an unfamiliar cultural context.

Although **qualitative methods** do not enable links to be identified and weighted with accurately indicated probability, they do enable plausible links to be explained and their significance to be understood, which is not possible with quantitative methods. While the interpretation of quantitative results depends entirely on the evaluator's interpretation and on the quantity of complementary qualitative information he processes, the qualitative study is geared to explaining possible links from the outset. From a strictly scientific point of view, however, the qualitative study cannot prove the existence of these links.

Another advantage of qualitative methods is their greater flexibility, in that knowledge acquired during the research process can have some influence on the continuing surveys. This enables more extensive knowledge to be acquired, and as a result of the inductive approach the researcher or evaluator sees himself as a learner and part of a social and communicative process (Flick et al. 1991, p. 170).

Qualitative surveys are more likely to ensure that account is taken of specific situations or individuals' different perceptions. However, this strength of qualitative methods is also their weakness. Their pronounced specificity results in generalizations often being impossible and in a degree of arbitrariness and uncontrollability emerging. This danger can best be averted with a systematic and transparent approach in a qualitative analysis.

Quantitative thinking having dominated empirical social research until well into the 1970s, the trend in all branches of research in the social sciences and also evaluation research has since been towards the qualitative methods.[18] Qualitative thinking is based on the call for the people "researched" to stop being passive and to play a more active part and on the goal of coming closer to them through interpretation as well as description. Pragmatic considerations regarding the differences in the time consumed, which is usually less in the case of the qualitative methods, have also played a part in the "qualitative change" in evaluation research.

Nonetheless, even in evaluation research and social analysis it does not seem wise to forgo quantification as a general rule, since in some cases it can be used very profitably. Hypotheses drawn up on the basis of qualitative studies can, for example, be purposefully backed by supplementary quantitative analyses. This approach would enable both the greater internal validity of quantitative analyses to be exploited and the production of quantities of irrelevant data to be avoided and time and money to be saved.

In the empirical investigation carried out here a qualitative approach is initially adopted. Building on this, quantification is undertaken on the basis of ordinally scaled scores. They enable the situations in various villages to be compared, but do not permit any absolute statements to be made. Given a sufficiently high number of village surveys, the methodology as conceived would permit a qualitative typification of villages on the basis of their performance or even variance analyses to be carried out with the help of statistical procedures.

4.6   Formation and Weighting of Indicators

In quantitative evaluations in particular indicators are often used to describe the degree of goal achievement or identify impacts. Indicators are meant to indicate something that cannot otherwise be observed or measured and are thus used primarily for quantification. The choice of indicators provides clues to the assumptions on which an argument is based. If the subject of a country's development, for example, is measured solely with gross national product per capita as the indicator, the likelihood is that the concept of development is defined in purely economic terms. The measurement of human development by means of indicators in UNDP's Human Development Report (HDR) in the 1990s has made a particular contribution to the revival of the debate on indicators in the development sphere. However, this debate primarily concerns the highly aggregated level at which comparisons of countries are made.[19]

In qualitative surveys indicators are used as a quantifying complement. If they are of a purely qualitative nature, they are better referred to as criteria.[20] Indicators and criteria enable impacts to be measured or assessed by reference to selected characteristics. There are many scientific publications on the problem of forming and weighting indicators, which will not be analysed in this study. Instead, fundamental aspects of selection and weighting are briefly discussed in the following, and the MAPP approach is then explained.

The quality and suitability of an indicator depend on a number of properties, such as its validity, reliability, relevance, sensitivity and specificity. For practical use it is also extremely important for an indicator to be measurable, available and useful. Which indicator is chosen also depends on what it costs and how long it takes to collect the necessary data. Above all, this means that an indicator must actually enable features of a concept that can be observed empirically to be inferred (validity). For such complex concepts as development, the difficulty with choosing indicators in the quantitative approach is to make the smallest and yet most representative choice for the measurement of a concept. In the HDR, for example, only three (or four, because one indicator is a combination of two) indicators are selected to form the Human Development Index. A commitment to a larger number of indicators would cause problems because of the absence of comparable statistics and engender excessive complexity.

A problem frequently encountered when indicators are to be chosen is therefore their partiality, i.e. indicators represent only a section of the concept, not its totality. However, an indicator may also measure more than it was actually intended to (lack of specificity). The values may then change because of factors other than those ascribed in the design. On the other hand, the indicators chosen may turn out to be incorrect or irrelevant (lack of relevance), or they may not react to minor changes (lack of sensitivity). If their suitability is to be continually reviewed, it is therefore important to make the reasons for the choice and weighting of indicators transparent in each case.

If, however, the evaluation is designed to be qualitative, there is no need for so severe a reduction to a few indicators. Increasingly, criteria regarded by those concerned as relevant to them are established.[21] For social analysis in particular Downing (1991; quoted from Kingsbury / Brown / Poukouta 1995, p. 25) refers to other important points of reference for the choice of indicators. As far as possible they should indicate trends that can still be influenced by operations and point to specific operations for particularly vulnerable groups. They should also be consistent in themselves, i.e. concern the whole year, for example, and be easy to interpret so that decisions may be taken quickly.

To enable comparisons to be made, indicators are typically measured at different strengths and at different scale levels. In the case of social analysis at project level the values are likely to be at nominal or ordinal scale level and are therefore only partly suitable for a quantitative analysis. If different indicators are needed for the description of a criterion, they can be combined to form an index. This presupposes the formation of a yardstick for the various indicators. Forming an index also calls for the weighting of the indicators, at least when the indicators do not correlate positively with one another. Like the choice of indicators, weighting is usually a matter of subjective discretion.

In the impact analysis method described in the empirical part of this study it is assumed that the lives of the target group change. It is important in this context to begin by defining criteria capable of indicating a social change of this kind. It is assumed that the social situation in a region or village cannot be described by means of one or a few metrically measurable indicators, but that a number of qualitative criteria are needed.

On the basis of this multidimensional understanding the four key social processes referred to by the ODA are taken as the basis for the evaluation design, as explained in the second chapter. A number of subcriteria appropriate for this purpose on sector-related grounds and of particular interest to the evaluation team are now allocated to the four criteria, referred to as key processes here. The second step is to reduce the criteria to bare essentials or to add further, essential criteria together with domestic and foreign project staff. In the test case the number of criteria was limited to 12.[22] After the target group has been given another opportunity to add to and correct these criteria, it is now assumed in the analysis that these 12 criteria, taken together, adequately describe all key social processes of the people in the project region and provide information on the essential aspects of the quality of life in the region.

As the ODA presuppose, it is assumed here again that social development cannot be described with just one indicator, but that several are needed. The relatively uniform development of all the criteria is an indication of robust, i.e. invulnerable, development, although it is far from being proof of this. Neither the concept of the four key social processes nor the SRL-concept, however, says any more on the question of the weighting of the criteria.

In the analysis undertaken here it is assumed that the various social criteria do not have a stable weight or have a stable importance attached to them for the life in a social community, but that they are of changing importance for the quality of life, depending on which factor happens to be at the minimum level. The author cites Liebig's law of limiting factors as an analogy (Finck 1992, pp. 24 ff.). This law states that the level of the yield produced by a plant is defined by the plant nutrient that is in shortest supply. To illustrate this, Liebig makes the following comparison: *"The water level in a barrel cannot rise any higher than the shortest stave."* Applied to the social situation, this means that the quality of life cannot be higher than the factor in the shortest supply. It follows from this: **only when all key social processes are optimal can the full human potential be realized. And a further conclusion: weightings and indices in the social sphere always relate to specific situations.**

Nor, if this comparison is taken as a basis, is it possible to rank or weight the various social criteria according to their importance for the quality of life, just as it is not possible to do so for the various plant nutrients in Liebig's model. Instead, the factor that is in shortest supply always determines the yield or, here, the quality of life. To extend this idea further, the goal of village development projects should therefore be to ensure that the various development factors are not overly hampered by one completely neglected factor. Moreover, certain positive effects can develop only if other factors have already been raised above the minimal level. The contents of projects excessively reduced to set operations would not therefore be very promising, unless other donors are also present and are able to close the gaps.

The analogy with the law of limiting factors means that below a certain threshold any factor is capable of causing the whole system to collapse. But how can a social collapse be defined? It is seen here as the disintegration of social cohesion, which can be gauged by whether people remain in their social context or detach themselves from it and leave, i.e. migration begins in the region. In this analysis migration is used as an indicator of whether life in the given social context is still tolerable or opportunities for development exist. Even though migration proves to be suitable as an indicator in this specific case, it need not be in other cases or in other regions. Migrations presuppose that destinations are available and that information on their existence is accessible. This is the case in the test example, since it has something of a tradition of migration.

4.7   Data Collection Methods

4.7.1   Conventional Methods

Data are collected for evaluations quite generally with the help of social science methodology. However, it is very common today to resort solely to the analysis of secondary material because of the shortage of time for evaluations (indirect methods). It is generally agreed, on the other hand, that some forms of data collection (direct methods) can improve the quality of evaluations and that a combination of the two approaches is desirable.[23]

When secondary material is evaluated, the study is extended from the literature in general to include project documents and local data collected for other purposes, which are analysed with the objective of the evaluation in mind. The most important documents are usually project applications and reports, any M&E system documents that may exist, the results of planning and ZOPP sessions, project, progress and similar reports and local statistics. Any opinions and evaluations relating to regionally or sectorally similar projects, topographical maps, aerial photographs, archive material and, of course, libraries and databases can also be of inestimable value for evaluation.

The most common methods of direct data collection for evaluations are surveys and inquiries, based on questionnaires, interviews, observations or direct measurements. A distinction needs to be made between oral and written, standardized and non-standardized inquiries, and between cross-section and panel surveys. The broader and more systematic such surveys are designed to be (random selection, random sampling, random sample surveys, full surveys), the more expensive and time-consuming they are. In development cooperation baseline surveys and surveys of representative households and firms are well-known. They are undertaken, for example, where the skills and opinions of larger target groups or a wide range of facts, structures and features are to be analysed. In the developing country context most surveys consist of interviews based on standardized questionnaires. This instrument is particularly suitable for statistical and quantitative evaluations and is thus able to identify and weight significant connections, which no other survey method is able to do on this scale. Such surveys have a tendency to produce some superfluous data, which are not all needed to get the most relevant information. On cost grounds alone it is therefore important to concentrate on data that are really important for the project. A sufficiently large random sample is, however, needed for a clean statistical analysis.

Interviews are important for both quantitative and qualitative approaches. Accordingly, they may be structured, semi-structured and unstructured or narrative. Semi-structured interviews, which are conducted by an interviewer with the help of a manual, are preferred and most frequently used for evaluations because they are fairly limited in scale and suitable for the goal-oriented approach. They are more flexible than closed-end interviews and also leave more scope for answers. This permits the collection of new and unexpected information that might have remained concealed in closed-end interviews. The disadvantage of highly unstructured interviews, on the other hand, is that they take a long time to evaluate and entail a heightened risk of errors as a result.

A distinction can be made between group and individual interviews, discussion with experts or with key informants. In project evaluations the information acquired usually undergoes qualitative analysis. The use of interviews enables both descriptive information to be collected and motivations and values to be understood. However, the interview is above all suitable for the creative development of proposals for solutions to problems and for new aspects that have not hitherto been considered. As the aim in practice is to reduce the number of interviews to the "optimum" level, the selection of key information is an important preliminary task. Kumar has, among other things, discussed and emphasized the opportunities presented by the interview when used in development cooperation (Kumar 1996b.). The following ways of selecting interview partners can be cited:

Table 3:	Selection and types of random sample in qualitative procedures
Types	**Definition**
Selection on the snowball principle	A key informant is first selected. He gives the names of other people who can provide further helpful information.
Selection on the basis of pertinent criteria	The selection is made on the basis of the principle of achieving the widest possible variance by choosing people with different functions or in different situations as far as possible.
Selection on the basis of quotas or proportions	The selection is made with a view to having representatives of all social groupings according to their importance in the social system, thus enabling weightings to be undertaken.
Random selection	A person come across by chance is selected.
Source: Narayan (1996), quoted from World Bank (no year), p. 6	

In addition to questionnaire-based surveys and interviews, observations – originally the conventional instrument of ethnology – are particularly important for evaluations. A distinction is made particularly between direct and participatory observation. The instrument is primarily suitable for explaining connections in certain complex behavioural patterns or situations. Observation is therefore well suited to complementing quantitative surveys and interviews. Participatory observation in particular also enables ways of life and sequences of actions to be experienced holistically, thus giving evaluators unfamiliar with the culture a chance of gaining a deeper understanding of courses of action. The problem with this instrument if it is to be used comprehensively in development cooperation is, however, that long periods of observation are needed, which is usually impossible in the case of evaluations, and that perception and interpretation problems arise particularly if the instrument is not used systematically. Observation therefore tends to be used in development cooperation in an unstructured form as a complementary instrument or for the clarification, or prior clarification, of specific questions, with observation criteria or categories being taken as a basis for certain situations.

4.7.2   Participatory Methods

Already in the late 1970s dissatisfaction with evaluation reports drawn up on the basis of conventional data collection methods, and especially quantitative surveys, which were expensive and even then sometimes lacked validity, led to the search for methods that cost less and were closer to reality. In 1981 Collinson described how a reliable study could be made without difficulty as part of an exploratory inquiry in only one week without the quality of the survey suffering as a result. In the ensuing years workshops at the Institute for Development Studies (IDS) in Sussex and fundamental articles by Chambers (1981), Belshaw (1981) and Carruthers & Chambers (1981) initially led to growing acceptance of what was known as **Rapid Rural Appraisal (RRA)**.[24]

RRA is subject to certain rules. The composition of the team, for example, is changed daily to ensure a maximum of different backgrounds to knowledge acquired and of different angles. If an RRA is to succeed, it is essential to limit the focus of study to important aspects. The team uses a set of simple, non-standardized methods to collect information and analyse data, which extends from semi-structured interviews and joint inspection of the locality through direct observation to analytical games.

Building on RRA, participatory inquiry methods were also devised during the development of participatory approaches to research which has been described above. They do not fundamentally differ from conventional methods. However, they are based on a different concept, which leads, among other things, to a change of approach to data collection and of the analysis and depiction of results. Participatory methods may include conventional elements and vice versa. This is very often the case, for example, with group interviews and group discussions. The same is true of systematic inspections of the locality or "transects". They are among the important instruments used for both procedures, the conventional and the participatory.

Within the participatory approach Participatory Rural Appraisal (PRA) is the best known method today.[25] PRA conforms to the general thinking on participatory procedures and sets particular store by joint learning and the recognition of local life as the basis for joint planning and action. This process is described as sharing realities. PRA is based on certain key concepts that account for its nature and lead to the typical approaches to description (Schönhuth / Kievelitz 1993, pp. 8 ff.). The most important are:

— **Triangulation**
   A form of cross-checking in relation to the composition of the team, sources of information and techniques used. On every team, for example, several disciplines and various fields of knowledge should be represented and there should be a balanced ratio of men to women. Every phenomenon should be examined from different angles and studied with different techniques.

— **Learning from and with people**
   The team should attempt as far as possible to see problems through the eyes of those concerned. The study instruments are used together; the focus is on the communal learning process.

— **Optimal ignorance and appropriate inaccuracy**
   The team avoids unnecessary accuracy when collecting data. Research and analysis continue only as long as needed for the recognition of needs or targeted activity.

PRA uses a basket of informal, but structured survey tools. Besides the formation of indicators, the analysis of secondary sources and the conducting of interviews (i.e. instruments that are also used in conventional evaluations), there is a range of typical PRA tools that can be used in various forms. Tools that are suitable for evaluations are summarized in the following:[26]

— **Transects and group walks**
   The study area is systematically examined together with informants for variable aspects (e.g. from North to South), and simple maps are compiled on this basis.

— **Seasonal calendar**

— **Maps of the social structure, social relations and decision-making processes** (social mapping, decision trees, VENN diagrams)
   These provide information on housing structures and conditions, public infrastructure and the social situation of households. Social mapping also includes sociograms.

— **Ranking techniques** (establishment of hierarchies of problems or lists of priorities, wealth ranking, social stratification)
These are important analytical tools for obtaining qualitative information on problems, preferences and also the incomes or prosperity of individual members of the community.

— **Timetables and historical trends**
These are used to provide a simple visualization of key historical events and perceived, crucial changes.

— **Contrasting comparisons**
Group A is, for example, asked to analyse Group B and vice versa. This method is often used in gender-oriented PRAs: the men and women separately estimate the women's workload, and the two estimates are then compared.

— **Gender-related analytical tools**[27]
"Gender analysis – access to resources" is used to provide information on the access of members of the household to resources and their control over such resources. "Women's time management" is used to provide information on their workloads, the time involved and the perception of the duration of burdens.

— **Acquiring the ability to analyse problems/evaluation training/knowing the degree of participation**
"Critical incident analysis" is used to develop the target group's analytical skills. The tool "Understanding the decision-making process" encourages the inhabitants to analyse decision-making processes and their opportunities for participating. With "Women's confidence" it is possible to measure the degree of women's participation and their self-confidence and change over time. The "Sarar resistance to change continuum" can help to increase the evaluation team's or project staff's awareness of the need to understand target groups' opposition to innovations and changes.

As the list shows, there are quite a number of tools that also seem interesting in the context of social impact analysis.

The question of how the various tools might be tailored and combined for social impact analysis to ensure a maximum of information and realism cannot be answered in this way, however. For this a design consisting of several instruments and geared specifically to impact analysis is needed. A set of instruments of this kind is developed in the empirical part of this study.

5   MAPP, a New Method of Social Impact Analysis

In the following part of the study a new method of analysing the social impact of poverty-oriented development programmes and projects close to target groups is presented. It is known as the method of impact assessment of poverty alleviation projects (MAPP). What is new about MAPP is the modification, the linking and combination of existing concepts and tools in a specific way to give a standardizable system that can be used in practice without undue expense.

As already mentioned, MAPP was developed on the basis of the effect model adopted by GTZ's Internal Evaluation Team and of the ODA's key social processes. By analogy with the law of limiting factors it was assumed that the social situation in a community can be described only with the help of several criteria which are not, moreover, subject to any fixed or absolute weighting of the various indicators. On the basis of this understanding the four key social processes to which the ODA refers:

— improvement or impoverishment of livelihoods,

— access to or exclusion from resources,

— expansion or reduction of knowledge,

— participation in or alienation from rights,

were considered and defined for the resource protection sector. The subcriteria were attributed in the way described earlier (see section 4.4). Five evaluation tools that build on each other were then combined to form an inquiry set, which was used to collect the basic data for the evaluation of social development in a rural project region. The combination of the context-related data obtained in this way and project-related input, output and outcome data permits statements to be made on project impacts.

The empirical test run was carried out taking the evaluation of a large-scale resource management programme (PGRN) in Mali as an example. The purpose of the test run was to assess feasibility, expense and the informative value of the conclusions that can be drawn with MAPP. During the test run the method was also adjusted to practical needs.

The following sections begin by presenting the evaluation design taken as a basis and explaining the survey and evaluation method. The substantive results of the test run are then discussed. The chapter ends with some deliberations on the method and the practical use of MAPP.

5.1   The Evaluation Concept of MAPP

5.1.1   Objectives of MAPP

MAPP pursues the following objectives:

(1) Social development in the daily lives of the target groups is to be depicted in a differentiated way.

(2) The effort involved in and the direct benefit of the project measures are to be identified through the eyes of various target and population groups.

(3) The social impacts of the project measures are to be made visible and comparable.

MAPP was developed for practical use by donor and counterpart organizations and is designed to meet the following requirements:

(1) **Simplicity**
Local experts are in principle to be able to carry out evaluations independently in cooperation with the target groups. MAPP is meant to be comprehensible to illiterate target groups.

(2) **Maximum informative value, transparency and validity of data**
It is to be possible to make unambiguous statements on trends and

impacts, and the origin of the statements is to be highly plausible and transparent.

(3) **Limited collection and evaluation effort**
Evaluation costs are to be kept as low as possible, and the time involved is also to be acceptable to the target group.

(4) **Satisfactory comparability of results**
The results are to be as schematic as possible so as to improve comparability, but this is to be accompanied by the least possible loss of information.

The idea behind MAPP is not that it should be possible to produce accurate measurement data. The evaluation effort involved would be far too great for this, and such data would not take account of the dynamics of social processes. Instead, reliable process-oriented tools are applied indicating social trends. Data are to be collected at no great expense and within a reasonable period so that changes in project management or important environmental factors leave their mark on the observation of impacts as soon as possible.

5.1.2   Description of the Evaluation Design

The evaluation design is essentially based on hypothetical "before-and-after comparisons" of actual life in the project region based on the systematized remembrance of the target groups. MAPP does not need preliminary investigations into the social situation already undertaken in the region. The dynamics of social development is taken into account with the design through the separate evaluation of each year in the project cycle. During the assessment absolute values are less important than relative values. The main factor is the description of the trend from one year to the next and the factors that cause this trend.

The primary analysis is carried out during **group discussions** conducted with representatives of the target groups. To increase the ability of the target groups to remember and to be sure of statements, the discussion begins with a reference to that year's special events, which all the participants remember well. Only when this has produced an "internal matrix" in all concerned are the various years evaluated by consensus.

Social development in the village is determined with the aid of a "social trend analysis", which covers a period of some twenty years and during which the twelve social sub-criteria are evaluated. The evaluation is based on a five-point scale ranging from "very negative" to "very positive". Points are again awarded for each year and criterion, and all changes are also explained in qualitative terms.

The **isolation of project impacts** from external factors is achieved with the help of several points of reference. The most important, however, is the target groups' perception, which is determined with the aid of two tools. A "life line" is first used to identify the minimum factor for the quality of life in the region. In the present case this factor is external and independent of the project. With the help of an "influence matrix" the relationships between project activities and social development are then evaluated on the pattern of the "paper computer" in Vester's "sensitivity model".[1] Direct observation, i.e. a systematic village walk and appraisal of physically visible project measures, enables the data provided by the target groups to be seen in perspective, i.e. compared with the evaluation team's view.

To enable the **internal validity** and **sensitivity** of the data collected in this way to be assessed, the test run also includes the simulation of a "with-and-without comparison". The findings in a village with which cooperation has recently begun are compared with the findings in project villages with which cooperation has been under way for some years. The indications gained from this comparison are, however, impaired by "disturbance factors", since in one year of cooperating with the PGRN the "without" village received considerable assistance, which has already had an impact in some respects. It also transpired during the inquiry that the village had been cooperating with the Norwegian organization PIDEB since 1988, which had also left visible traces. These circumstances are taken into account in the interpretation of the data.[2]

MAPP includes **several appraisal steps**, mostly undertaken by the target groups themselves, which enable statements to be made – on the basis of the lives of the target groups – on the social impact of a specific project. The various steps are described in the following sections.

If the project administration service also has input, output and outcome data, the ratio of social costs to social benefits can be determined from the MAPP findings by means of a simple comparison. With the help of output data the project operations can also be assessed quantitatively for the impact they have had. Outcome data also enable the technical and social benefits of operations to be compared. Where all types of data are available, the "social efficiency" can thus be compared.

It should be borne in mind, however, that these are not technical data but data on criteria relating to the quality of life and that evaluating them from an economic angle does not seem entirely appropriate.[3] As already explained above, the various social trends cannot be weighted in any sequence, since this would very quickly give rise to absurd and undignified considerations.[4/5]

5.2   Data Collection and Evaluation Methodology

The MAPP data collection methodology is based on a set of tools which includes participatory as well as conventional tools. To ensure that the data are sufficiently valid and reliable, the triangulation principle is adopted, i.e. particularly important areas of information are surveyed twice and with different tools.

The main inquiry method used for data collection and evaluation is the group discussion. Although the group discussion also forms part of the repertoire of classical methods, of course, the PRA methodology is deliberately used through the visualization of all findings and their iterative preparation, analysis, adjustment and, ultimately, recording in a set pattern in a form that is as comprehensible as possible to all members of the target group.

The unit analysed in this case is "the village", represented by the various participants in the discussion. The size of the discussion group is not fixed and comprised between 20 and 40 participants during the test run. As access to the group is open during the MAPP sessions, the number of participants may fluctuate during the analysis.

The following table illustrates the approach adopted:

Table 4:   The various MAPP phases

Preparatory phase	
1)	Adjustment of some elements of MAPP to project sector, region and characteristics of the target groups
2)	Development of a set of social sub-criteria with the project staff as suggestion for the target groups

⇩

Implementation phase	
1	**Evaluation of social development and project impact with the target groups**
1.1	Life line
1.2	Trend analysis
1.2.1	Definition of the social sub-criteria
1.2.2	Assessment of the social trend
1.3	Activity list
1.4	Influence matrix
2	**Observations by the evaluation team**
2.1	Transect (systematic village walk)
2.2	Situational analysis

⇩

Phase of data analysis	
1)	Establishment of the development and impact profile
2)	Comparison of the findings of the participatory evaluation with the conclusions drawn during direct observation
3)	Comparison of the findings with M&E data, project documents and any additional information obtained

For the validity of the data it is important to ensure that representatives of all relevant social and socio-professional groups participate and that the group is as heterogeneous as possible in terms of gender, age and social status. The evaluation team can influence the composition of the group by stating when the visit to the village is announced that an appropriately mixed group is wanted. If it is actually to attend the meeting as such, it is – if the Sahelian region is concerned – important not only to choose the dry season for the meeting, because little work is done in the fields during this period, but also to take account of the specific and often tight timetable observed by the women and possibly divergent timetables of other social groups. Whether all social groups participate in the evaluation together or whether it is better to carry out separate evaluations depends on whether the vulnerable and disadvantaged groups are able to have their say at a mixed meeting of this kind. This in turn depends on the group's integrative strength, the evaluation team's skills and the socio-cultural conditions in the society concerned. As any division of the group doubles the time and effort involved, it should be considered very care-fully. However, different perceptions by different social groups can be also reported in mixed sessions, e.g. by visualising different assessments with different colours.

The actual evaluation time needed for MAPP is eight to ten hours per unit analysed. Two days must therefore be set aside for a visit to a village or discussion group, when the time spent travelling to and from the village, the time spent waiting, the time devoted to the introductory discussion and lunch breaks are taken into account.

After the purpose of the evaluation has been explained and discussed at the beginning of the group meeting, the social criteria on which the evaluation is to be based are proposed by the evaluation team and sup-plemented and corrected by the target groups. The various tools are then used. With the first four tools data on the social development of the village and the significance of the project operations are collected. At first an appropriate matrix is drawn on a board (see below), and the tool concerned is explained or the task is set in such a way that everyone can understand. After this the discussion and the awarding of points are left to the target group, without frequent intervention. The ongoing discussion is translated for the external team members in the background in such a way that the proceedings are disturbed as little as possible. If the group awards points in a way which is not immediately comprehensible, ques-tions are asked and the explanations are noted. If individual social groups fail to agree on the points to be awarded, the evaluation team should react flexibly, for example, by making a separate record of the divergent opinion. Where the awarding of points by the target groups does not seem logical, they are asked to explain. In some cases this may reveal misunderstandings, in others the evaluation team may come to understand the target groups' initially incomprehensible assessments.

The fifth tool is a systematic village walk (transect), during which the evaluation team accompanied by some members of the target groups examine all physically visible project operations for their dimensions and soundness. This transect performs a monitoring function, since it enables differences between the target groups' and the evaluation team's perceptions to be identified.

The various instruments are explained in greater detail in the following:

---

(1)   "Life line" ⇒ **identification of minimum factors and evaluation of general conditions**

Description: The target groups are asked to draw a curve showing how their community has developed over the past 20 years. The amplitudes of the curve indicate the change in quality of life. The scale has five levels, comprising evaluation units from "very negative" to "very positive". The criterion that determines how many points are awarded determines the minimum factor, which is fixed at the beginning, but may be questioned and changed for other years. The aim in each case is explicitly to refer to the rating criterion, to record it and to justify every amplitude anew. Figures 6, A1 and A2 show examples of life lines.

Explanation: This strongly context- and process-oriented tool is suitable for the initial evaluation situation and is easy for the target groups to set up. The life line shows what factors are within the minimum range for the people in a period they themselves determine. This provides a first clue to the significance of the "external factors", the community environment, and also an indication of whether or not they are within the project's radius of action.

Duration: About 1½ hours

(2)   "Social trend analysis" ⇒ **establishment of a matrix on social development**

Description: On the basis of the initially established sub-criteria relating to the four key social criteria and with the aid of a "social trend analysis" a detailed profile of the village is drawn, and it is shown how it has changed within the project cycle (or over a longer period). A five-level evaluation scale from "very negative" to "very positive" is again prescribed for the group to evaluate every year. If the number of points awarded changes from one year to the next, the reasons for the change are discussed and recorded. Examples of trend analyses can be found in Figures 4, A1 and A2.

Explanation: This likewise context- and process-oriented tool produces a picture of the social development in the various villages and reflects the **gross impact** of the project to be evaluated. It is the most important basis for the preparation of the influence matrix.

Duration: About 3 hours

(3)   "Activity list" ⇒ **identification of the importance and beneficiaries of project activities and of the workload and expenses involved**

Description: With the aid of a simple chart, again based on a five-level scale, all project activities and the pertinent project sponsors are noted. The importance of each activity for the daily lives of the target groups is then rated, and the group benefiting from the activity is identified. Points are then awarded for the workload and financial input required for the implementation and maintenance of the operations. Examples of activity lists can be seen in Figures 3, A3 and A4.

Explanation: The "activity list" is a project-oriented and snapshot tool and gives an overview of the activities and project sponsors in the village and of the various groups of beneficiaries. Above all, this enables the project being examined to be compared with other projects in terms of perceived importance and their spread throughout the community to be determined. A "cost-benefit comparison" can also be made, the importance of an operation for the daily lives of the target groups being compared with the workload it has entailed. The chart also shows how fairly the package of measures is distributed among the beneficiary groups.

Duration: About 1½ hours.

(4)   "Influence matrix" ⇒ **attribution of impacts of project activities**

Net impacts are now attributed systematically with the aid of a matrix in which the strength of the influence of each project activity on each social criterion is again rated on a scale of one to five. By analogy with Vester's "paper computer", active and passive totals reflecting, respectively, the most influenced social criterion and the most influential project activity are finally formed. Examples are shown in Figures 6, A5 and A6.

Explanation: The influence matrix links the context view with the project view, and, like the activity list, it is a snapshot of the actual situation. If valid data are to be obtained, it is important for the target groups' attention to be drawn to the fact that what are needed are not hypothetical but actually identifiable influences, both direct and indirect.

Duration: About two hours

(5)   "Transect" ⇒ **cross-section of the community**

All visible project measures in the community are inspected by the evaluation team for effectiveness, e.g. magnitude and soundness. The impression gained by the evaluation team is compared with the impression of the various measures previously conveyed by the target groups.

Especially where the evaluation team spends the night in the village, it has ample opportunity to gain further insights into life in the community. If its members are already familiar with the region and, to some extent, the target groups' living conditions, they can achieve this systematically with no major effort by using the social criteria virtually as an inner yardstick to evaluate the observations while they are being made. A kind of journal can be kept of these observations, so that the notes taken during the appraisal phase may be compared with the target groups' statements.

Duration: Varies widely. The cross-section may take several hours, depending on the number and accessibility of the measures.

Establishment of a development and impact profile ⇒ appraisal of the evaluation meeting

The further, summary appraisal and establishment of a development and impact profile occur during an ex post assessment phase. This is based on the records of the matrices established in the community. The profile is used for summarizing the most important information on each community (or each survey unit) on a sheet of paper in such a way that rapid comparisons are possible. The development of the profiles can be seen in Tables 9 to 11. The point of departure is again formed by the key social processes, to which the sub-criteria are attributed. The rating system (e.g. points system) used in the evaluation with the target groups is recoded into a numbers system. All the values falling within the project period are now transferred from the matrix to the social trend analysis. The trend for each criterion, deduced from the course of events each year, is also entered on the scale of one – "very negative" – to five – "very positive". Stable differences from the initial year of one step are rated with "+" or "–". Where the points jump two or more steps and remain stable for several years, they are marked "++" or "--". Linking the various points along the criteria produces a vertical trend line indicating overall development. If the line more or less coincides with the "+/-"rating line, there has been no fundamental social development in the village. If the course followed by this line is very uneven, the social development in the village has not been very robust or is highly vulnerable. If the line has a uniform tendency to the right, a positive development is discernible; a uniform tendency to the left allows of the opposite conclusion. The trend lines are particularly suitable for comparing different results obtained from several inquiry units. The next column, on the other hand, contains qualitative statements by the target groups on the causes of the processes of change, which allow of interpretative conclusions. The statements are derived from the records of the discussions during the compilation of the various matrices and lists. Finally, an entry is made in a separate column to indicate which organization has played a major role in causing the trends or whether external, i.e. uninfluenced, factors are responsible. The data required for this are obtained from the activity lists and life lines.

5.3   MAPP Test Run

5.3.1   The *Projet de Gestion des Ressources Naturelles* (PGRN)

The PGRN, in which the method was put to the test, is a resource management programme financed by the World Bank and supported by the GTZ. The counterpart is Mali's Ministry of Rural Development and the Environment. The PGRN began work in January 1991 and is scheduled to continue for 15 to 20 years. By the year 2000 the PGRN is to have reached 600 villages in 15 regions of Mali. The GTZ's contribution is limited to cooperation with 40 villages.

The aim of the programme is to contribute to village development with the aid of sustainable land use systems. The participatory development and implementation of land use plans is a core element in this context. Stopping or reversing the process of degradation is intended to safeguard agricultural yields and so to help alleviate poverty (overall goal).

The German contribution from the beginning of 1995 until the end of 1998 cost about DM 9.6m. The essential activities include the assignment of two long-term experts, local and international short-term consultants, the supply of limited quantities of material goods and local grants for the implementation of the land use plans and monitoring in the village communities participating.

Where the GTZ's work is concerned, the following basic principles apply to all operations:

— **participation** of the villagers in all decisive project activities, from planning to implementation;

— **holistic approach**, i.e. the networking of all operations undertaken through interdisciplinary work from the beginning of the project;

— **replicability** of the operations undertaken under the organizational and financial conditions prevailing in Mali;

— **sustainability** in the sense of safeguarding the productivity of natural resources, with account taken of social-economic conditions in the test areas.

On the basis of the experience gained in similar programmes a flow chart of the activities, beginning with the establishment of local administrative structures and the analysis of the problems, continuing with progressive land use planning and ending with the implementation of the land use plans, was developed. As the analysis and planning involved in the approach take about a year, whereas the people need solutions to some problems quickly, the PGRN attempted until 1995, in the context of "confidence-building measures", to solve pressing problems with simple, affordable operations before the planning process was completed. After an interim evaluation by World Bank consultants, however, these confidence-building measures were abandoned without any explanation being given.[6]

The actual land use planning in the villages is done with the aid of aerial photographs and maps prepared together with the target groups. The village community begins by determining the village boundaries and the parts of the area to be included in the plans. With village committees set up specially for this purpose forms of use that would be conceivable in certain circumstances in the future are added on the basis of the current forms of use. Each unit is discussed by the people and technicians before the allocation supported by the whole is eventually made. On this basis a land use plan which affects all uses and in which account is also taken of the village infrastructure is now developed. The contributions made by the various development partners are listed, and an attempt is made to implement these concepts by means of binding agreements or contracts between the participants. The work is usually performed and monitored by the people themselves. They are able to follow the progress of the work with the help of an M&E system at village level, they know what has been invested, and they are able to arrange for adjustments to be made to the plans at any time.[7]

5.3.2   Approach and Basic Information on the Villages Visited

Bafoulabé in western Mali was chosen to be the test region together with the project management. The region is about 400 km from Bamako and can be reached by a track which in places is passable only with difficulty. Bafoulabé was chosen because, unlike other regions nearer the capital, the PGRN is the "principal donor" there, and distinguishing the various donors was not considered to be very difficult. The evaluation team consisted of three and sometimes four people: one local project staff member of the PGRN, one external person (the author), a interpreter and the technical adviser responsible for the project region. Three of the ten project villages in the study region were selected. The selection criteria were the duration of cooperation with the project and the time the villagers could spare from their work. Prior personal visits were made to notify the villagers of the appraisal and to agree on a date.

Bafoulabé is situated in the transitional area between the Sahel and Sudan, where arable farming is threatened by constantly recurring periods of drought, the annual rainfall averaging about 600 - 700 mm, with the unequal distribution typical of the area. The villages visited – **Kalé**, **Ouassala** and **Damba** – are located near the River Senegal, which is a good source of irrigation water but not of drinking water, and near a railway line from the capital, Bamako, to Senegal. According to the advisers, the railway line has no more than a marginal influence on village life, since the tracks are 3 - 4 km from the villages and the trains do not as a rule stop there. It is therefore virtually impossible for trade in foodstuffs to develop, and the mobility of the people is no greater in the villages near the tracks than in those farther away, since a detour must always be made via Mahina, which has a railway station. The three villages chosen have between a few hundred (Damba and Kalé) and over a thousand inhabitants (Ouassala), and the population consists of several **socio-professional groups** belonging to different language groups in some cases. Farmers, mostly from the Malinké ethnic group, although the

Bambara, Soninké, Diawambé and Kassonké ethnic groups are also represented to a diminishing extent, form the largest population group. Some families of the minority ethnic groups go in for fishing as well as farming, whereas the Malinké never fish. Also living in the village is a significant number of Peulh, some of whom have settled, while others are nomadic and pass through the village area once or more a year, living there for a short time. Society is largely structured along Islamic and hierarchical lines. The "higher-placed" farmers and herders, who have a hierarchy based on age and gender, contrast with "caste members", who work as smiths, grios[8] or craftsmen.

The main crops grown in the region are foxtail millet, sorghum, maize and groundnuts. Irrigated vegetable and rice growing in the dry season is new and is supported by the PGRN. The region is a few kilometres north of the present limit for the growing of cotton.

While the **shortage of land** is not very pronounced in Bafoulabé, non-degraded land is already in short supply in some villages (including Kalé and Damba). Only men have the right to own land, the women being responsible for neither arable farming nor the protection of resources, they work in the fields to help their husbands and they do keep small animals. Access to firewood is a major problem in all the villages, the nearest stands of timber being 2 - 10 km away.

Of late the **school enrolment rate** among the children has been very high, over 90 %. All the children have been able to reach their schools on foot for some years. The number of literate adults, however, is very small, the villages evaluated differing widely in this respect. This is probably due to the varying distances to the nearest town, Bafoulabé, that today's adults would have had to cover in their childhood to reach the nearest school.[9]

A common and immediately apparent disease among adult men is **river blindness**: almost all the old men, i.e. the village decision-makers, are blind. Initially, this was detrimental to the study, which operates extensively with visualizations, and posed completely unexpected problems. In the course of the evaluation period, however, a kind of translation mechanism was developed for the blind, and some of those concerned played an active part in the discussion despite their handicap. The health of the **children** is affected primarily by meningitis and measles epidemics, which have caused serious problems in recent years and which will be considered later in the evaluation.

5.3.3   Results of the Test Run

The methodology is explained in the following, with the village of Kalé taken as an example, the results and matrices for the other villages being described in the annex.[10]

The Social Sub-criteria

Table 5 shows the twelve social sub-criteria used as indicators of social development in the region (see section 2.2).

Table 5: Social sub-criteria for the Bafoulabé test region			
Improvement or impoverishment of livelihoods	Access to or exclusion from resources	Expansion or reduction of knowledge	Participation in or alienation from rights
Family income	Access to firewood	School enrolment rate among the children	Conflicts over use of resources between farmers and herders and between men and women
Agricultural yields	Access to drinking water	Knowledge acquired of sustainable land use	
Health status of the children	Access to the market		
Consumer prices of grain	Access to fertile land		
	Access to means of transport		
Source: Jointly compiled by the PGRN project staff, the evaluation team in Bafoulabé and the target groups			

The Minimum Factors for Life Quality (Life Line)

Figure 5 shows the life line for Kalé, as drawn by the target groups.[11]

All the life lines reveal that by far the most common minimum factor on which the evaluation of the quality of life in all villages depends is the **quantity of rainfall**. The quantity of rainfall is regarded as directly proportional to the harvest that is available to the village and may determine survival. The curves in all the villages show that, because of the disastrous droughts affecting large parts of Africa, it was far more difficult to cope in the 1970s and 1980s than in the 1990s.

Apart from the distribution of rainfall, it is clear that very few events in certain years determine the general evaluation of the quality of life in the village. Only in Kalé are the celebration of several weddings after the return of the migrants in 1986 and the election of a democratic government in 1990 mentioned as favourable key events.[12] In Damba, apart from the shortage of rainfall, only one incident in 18 years was seen as having had an adverse effect on the communal quality of life.[13]

It is clear from the life lines that migration can be regarded as a direct consequence of serious droughts. In the 1990s it has been far less pronounced than in the 1970s and 1980s.

As regards the part played by the PGRN in the quality of life in the villages it was emphasized particularly in Kalé but also in Damba while the life lines were being drawn that the project, and especially the grain bank, had made it easier to cope with the fluctuations in rainfall, i.e. it had acted as a cushion.

The life lines generally show that the PGRN's influence on village development must be judged against the background of rainfall distribution and that this is the minimum determinant of life in the region. This is not to say, however, that because of this "disturbance factor" project impacts cannot become apparent. This would be likely only if rainfall was very low. In the case of normal rainfall fluctuations, on the other hand, project impacts are perceptible from minor peaks on the life line. The target groups claim that the project work has already had an impact of this kind in Kalé.

Figure 5: **Life line of Kalé village**

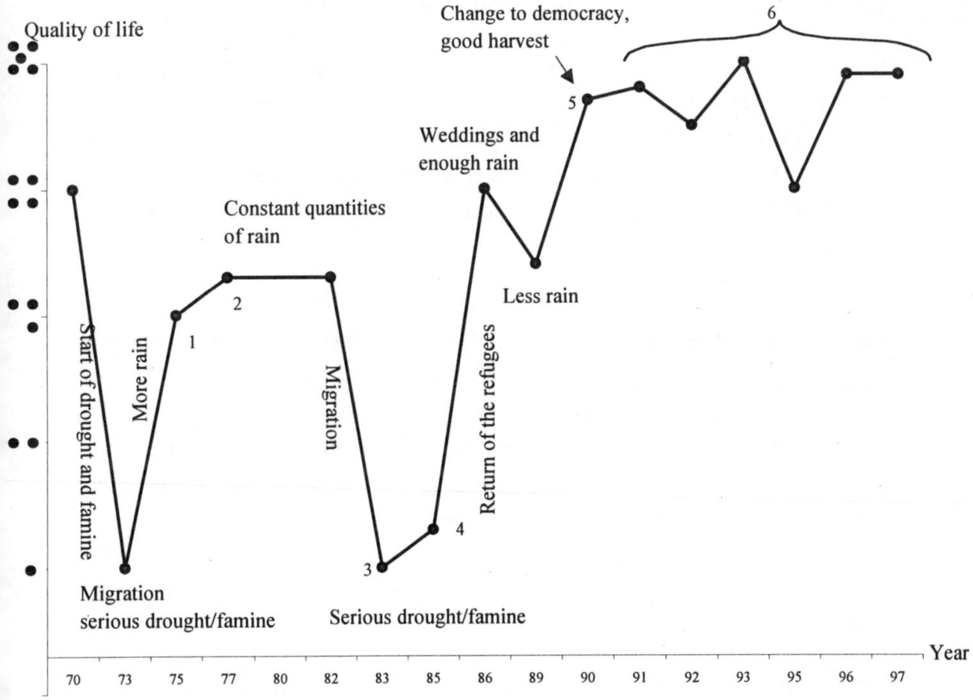

1: Despite sufficient rain, many fields could not be cultivated, since the people first had to return to the village.
2: The rainfall was insufficient, but there was food aid.
3: Migration of many young to Libya.
4: Somewhat better situation, since the migrants sent money to the village.
5: Democracy is helping and liberating us. For example, we can now cut wood without being punished.
6: Fluctuations in rainfall as otherwise, but greater buffer capacity for bridging period between one harvest and the next (e.g. grain bank).

Source: Description by the target groups in Kalé

Social Trends and Their Causes (Social Trend Analysis)

Table 6 now shows social development in Kalé related to all twelve criteria over a period of seven years.[14] This indicates clearly positive to very positive trends in all three villages in the 1990s.

It is evident that this trend is more pronounced within the project cycle in Kalé and Ouassala, the villages that have been cooperating with the PGRN for some time, than in Damba, the village that has joined the project more recently.[15] The main improvement in the last few years has been in **access to resources**. The target groups ascribe this improvement primarily to the work of the PGRN.[16]

The **knowledge** criteria have continued to develop positively over the project period. The target groups say they now know more about ways of using and protecting their area than they used to.[17] The **school enrolment rate** has also risen sharply in all the project villages in recent years. This trend is not, however, due to the PGRN's work, but to the construction of schools by other organizations as well as to a general growth of awareness that is evidently occurring in all villages. Another very important factor in this respect is the efficiency of the Mali authorities, which have sent teachers to all parts of the country and paid their salaries regularly since it became democratic.[18]

The social criteria that stand for the evaluation of **living standards**, on the other hand, have not developed in any clear direction. As mentioned above, agricultural yields in particular have so far been influenced more by external factors than by the PGRN's project work. Where family incomes are concerned, however, there are signs of a positive trend in the villages that have been involved in the project for some time, which the target group attributes to the PGRN's support (and especially to the grain bank and, secondly and thirdly, to irrigated vegetable growing and erosion prevention measures). In contrast, Damba, which has only just begun many of the project operations, complains that family incomes declined temporarily in 1997. The target groups put this down to the many fund-raising activities for the community projects that affected all families in that year.

Table 6:	Trend analysis for Kalé								
	Year	PGRN begins ↓							
Social Criteria	**1990**	**'91**	**'92**	**'93**	**'94**	**'95**	**'96**	**'97**	**Trend '92-'97**
Improvement or impoverishment of livelihoods									
Agricultural yields	••••	••••	•••••	••••	•••	••••	••••	•••	-
Family incomes	••	••	••	•••	••••	••••	••••	••••	++
Consumer prices of cereals	••••	••••	••••	••••	••••	••••	•	•••••	+
Health status of children	••••	••••	••••	••••	••••	•••	•	••	--
Access or exclusion from resources									
Access to firewood	•••	•••	•••	•••	•••	•••••	•••••	•••••	++
Access to drinking water	•	•	•	•	•	•••	•••	•••	++
Access to the market	•	•	•	•	•	••••	••••	••••	++
Access to means of transport	•	•	•	•	•	••••	••••	••••	++
Access to productive land	••••	••••	••••	•	••	•••	•••••	•••••	++
Expansion or reduction of knowledge									
School enrolment rate	•	•	•	•	•	•••••	•••••	•••••	++
Knowledge of sustainable land use	••	••	••	•••••	•••••	•••••	•••••	•••••	++
Participation in or alienation from rights									
Conflicts between farmers and herders[a]	•••	•••	•••	•••	•	•	•	•	--
Migration[b]	•	••	•	••••	••••	••••	••••	••••	++

Key:			Remarks:
•••••	=	very positive	a The higher the number of points, the fewer the conflicts.
••••	=	positive	b The higher the number of points, the less migration.
•••	=	fair	
••	=	negative	
•	=	very negative	

The trend in the **health status of the children** in two villages has, however, been extremely negative. This is due to several measles and meningitis epidemics in recent years. Despite the existence of a health station, the children were not vaccinated or treated early enough. Inadequate organization of the health services is presumably to blame. This should be investigated more closely at local level.[19]

In Kalé and Ouassala the **conflicts** between farmers and herders also grew during the project cycle, and in Damba's case relations between the two groups remained poor during this period. Directly associated with the PGRN project are conflicts caused by the creation of nature reserves, stone lines and newly established paths to be used by animals. According to the farmers in all three villages, these paths are ignored by the herders, even though they were defined in a joint negotiating process. The herders drive their animals through areas designated for other purposes, which are damaged as a result.

Although the concept of participatory land use planning, in which all socio-professional groups are involved, is meant to defuse such conflicts,[20] it has not so far succeeded. After making inquiries at project headquarters, the GTZ staff said that a method had not yet been found for the PGRN's work to enable a situation to be achieved in which the herders *actually* joined in the decision-making on land use planning and supported the decisions taken. Although rights of passage for the herders are included in the plans, land use planning is, in the final analysis, undertaken for the farmers and not for the herders. This unintentional preferential treatment of the farmers is already apparent from the fact that the planning unit for the projects is the area of the village inhabited by the farmers and not, say, the nomadic route followed by the herders or the areas used by both groups. This latter option would, however, presuppose that staff of organizations themselves understood the herders' seasonal nomadic movements or at least had an accurate knowledge of them.

The conflicts in the villages can be investigated only with indirect questions and skilful manoeuvring if the evaluation team is to avoid the anger of the whole village and seeing considerable blame laid at its door since, according to popular belief, asking direct questions causes conflict in itself. Information on the conflict situation should therefore be gathered by observation, and it should not be talked about too much. What conflicts exist are revealed sooner or later during the two-day group discussion. This presupposes, however, that the relevant parties to the conflict are present and form part of the same group.[21]

As the tables show, **migration** has declined in all the villages during the project cycle.[22] In the 1990s living conditions have already improved as a result of better rainfall, as the life lines of all villages reveal. In Ouassala, however, the "better" life and the fact that more people are staying in the villages are explicitly ascribed by the target group to the changes brought about by the PGRN.

Project Activities and Beneficiary Groups (Activity List)

Table 7 shows the activity list, taking Kalé as its example. The lists relating to the other villages are to be found in Tables A3 and A4 in the annex.[23]

The activity lists show that in all the villages many operations are assisted by various organizations. The majority of the operations are being supported by the PGRN. In Damba's case the Norwegian organization PIDEB also plays an important role. In all the villages the community projects, i.e. the school, the health station and the grain bank, are obviously very important to the villagers.[24] The existence of these services forms the basis for an intact social system, which benefits the whole population. If these services were not provided, the "productive operations" would hardly be capable of development. The participants in the discussion on the evaluation of the project activities were therefore always prone to say: *"La santé avant tout"*.

The "productive operations" and the "conventional resource protection operations" benefit only some of the villagers. In practical terms this means that **direct benefits are confined to men engaged in arable farming**. Because of their area of activity and their monopoly on land ownership they alone are interested in erosion prevention, and they alone buy donkey carts or have a right to buy them under the project rules.[25]

It is also male beneficiary groups of a fairly small size who are affected by the agricultural operations that are undertaken "quasi-privately" on the various holdings. They include, for example, such measures as improved poultry- and bee-keeping, for which only a few farms qualify because of

Table 7:	Activity list for Kalé			
Activity	Organization	Importance for daily life	Beneficiary group[a] Women (W) / Men (M)	Labour expended
Health station	OO[b]	•••••	M + W	•••
School	OO	•••••	M + W	•••
Nature reserves	PGRN	••••	M	•
Anti-erosion contour stone-lines	PGRN	••••	M	•••••
Composting facilities organic manuring	PGRN	••••	M	••••
Grain bank	PGRN	••••	M + W	•••
Sheep fattening	PGRN	•••	M + W	••
Village savings bank	OO (?)	•••	M + W	••
Irrigated rice growing	PGRN	•••	M + W	•••••
Irrigated vegetable grow-ing /irrigation plant	PGRN	•••	W	•••••
Pump for well	OO	••	M + W	•
Tree plantations	PGRN	•	M	••
Bee-keeping	PGRN	•	M	•

Key:
••••• = very important / very considerable expenditure of labour
•••• = important / considerable expenditure of labour
••• = fairly important / medium expenditure of labour
•• = little importance / little expenditure of labour
• ~ = no importance / no expenditure of labour

Remarks:
a   Where socio-professional groups are concerned, almost all the users are farmers.
b   Other organizations.

specific essential operating requirements and the limited demand for the products. They are therefore bound to continue to be of limited importance to the villagers as a whole, even though they may be very important to the individual farm.[26] Measures that can be undertaken both communally and on a private basis occupy an intermediate position. Specifically, these are, for example, irrigated vegetable and rice growing, the planting of trees and the creation of nature reserves. How rights of use and compulsory work are arranged will depend on the various plans. It has not been possible for any population group in any of the villages to derive the full benefit from these sometimes fairly large-scale and professionally designed operations because they have been in progress for a relatively short time or because of the long lead times they require.[27] They therefore play a relatively insignificant role in the evaluation. This will probably change very sharply in the years to come, since vegetable growing in particular seems destined – in the author's view – to be one of the most promising operations, given its scale and the methods employed.

According to the villagers, their contribution to the operations largely consists of their labour, less often of funding.[28] The work is generally performed by those who also derive benefit from the operation concerned, i.e. the non-nomadic men. In this respect the distribution is fair. Input is in proportion to benefit, except where the operations have not yet been running long enough to produce a yield, as in the case of the composting facilities in Damba and vegetable growing in Kalé, or have long lead times before their full benefit is enjoyed, as in the case of the tree plantations and nature reserves in all the villages.

The Impact of Project Operations on the Quality of Life (Influence Matrix)

The influence matrix (Table 8) and the corresponding matrices in the annex (Tables A5 and A6) show the qualitative influence of the various project activities on social development in the villages as perceived by the target groups. The figures indicate the perceived net influence of the activities, i.e. the external "disturbance factors" are not included as they are in the trend analysis.

A five-point system ranging from "0 = no influence" to "4 = very pronounced influence" was again taken as a basis. Once the matrix was completed, the row and column totals were formed. High row totals indicate criteria influenced by many project operations. The row totals can also be called passive totals. The column totals, on the other hand, indicate the activity that influences the most criteria. They are therefore known as active totals.

Table 8:   Influence matrix for Kalé

Social criteria		Organic manur-ing	conture stone-lines	Nature reserves	Vege-table/rice growing	Donkey carts	Well pump	Sheep fattening	Health station	Grain bank	Tree planting	Savings bank	School	Σ passive + 146 / - 9
								Project activities						
Improvement or impoverishment of livelihoods														
Family incomes		3	3	2[a]	3	4	0	4	0	3	0	1	-1[b]	+ 24 / - 1
Agricultural yields		4	4	1	3	4	2	3	0	3[c]	3	2[d]	0	+ 29
Health status of children		0	0	0	2[e]	4	4	0	4	0	0	2	0	+ 16
Access to or exclusion from resources														
Firewood		0	0	0	0	2	0	0	0	0	4	0	0	+ 6
Drinking water		0	0	0	0	0	4	0	0	0	0	0	0	+ 4
Market		-1	0	0	0	4	0	0	0	0	0	0	0	+ 5
Means of transport		0	0	0	0	4	0	0	0	0	0	1	0	+ 5
Fertile land		4	4	4	2	4	1	2	0	0	4	0	0	+ 25
Expansion or reduction of knowledge														
Sustainable land use		4	4	4	2	4	1	3	0	3	4	0	0	+ 29
School enrolment rate		0	0	0	0	0	0	0	0	0	0	0	4	+ 4
Participation or alienation from rights														
Land use conflicts[f]		0	0	- 4[g]	0	0	0	0	0	0	- 4	0	0	- 8
Migration[h]														
Σ aktive + 123 / -2		+ 16	+ 11 / - 4	+ 11	+ 15	+ 30	+ 12	+ 12	+ 4	+ 9	+ 15 / - 4	+ 6	+ 4 / - 1	

Remarks: The question asked during the discussion was always: How does the project activity x as it exists or operates in your village today influence social criterion y?

a   The fruits of wild trees and bushes are sold in the market.
b   School fees are a burden on the household budget.
c   The influence is indirect: we gain time because we are not constantly having to go to market. This means we have more time at home to till the fields.
d   As we have access to credit, we are able to invest.
e   The influence stems from the healthier diet due to the increase in the supply of vegetables.
f   Conflicts between herders and farmers.
g   The herders pass through the nature reserve with their herds, which has greatly increased the tension.
h   Data on the influence of the activities on migration were only collected in Damba and Ouassala.

Key:

0   =   no influence
1   =   slight influence
2   =   medium influence
3   =   pronounced influence
4   =   very pronounced influence

The sign '-' before a figure means a negative influence.

As all the tables reveal in the present case, **providing** the villagers **with donkey carts** is awarded the highest number of points in the column total. The specific allocation of points shows that donkey carts have a wide range of impacts on the social situation in the villages and constitute a **key measure**. Owning a donkey cart helps in various ways both to improve living standards and to facilitate access to resources.[29] It is not therefore surprising that conflicts occur when the use of donkey carts is a male preserve. As donkey carts can be put to many different uses and are the only means of transport in the villages, a wide range of opportunities would be opened up if women had the right to use or, better yet, to own them. The PGRN is therefore recommended to abandon its one-sided tying of the subsidization of the carts to erosion prevention measures or to complement this with a second link to women's activities. For their part, the women should try to learn how to use donkey carts, by applying to the PGRN for lessons, for example, if they intend to seize the opportunities that the carts present.[30]

The row totals in the tables show that the project activities have so far been particularly successful in improving **knowledge of sustainable land use systems**. According to the villagers, however, one or other project activity has had a positive impact on almost all of the other criteria. The trend analysis reveals, on the other hand, that so far **access to firewood** has been made hardly any easier. Although the use of donkey carts in the search for firewood is offsetting the shortage in two villages in the short term, the increased radius over which wood can be collected is simply hastening the desertification process in the longer term.[31] The negative outcome is due to the long growth periods of the trees planted with support from the project. Given the heavy demand for wood, the afforested areas also seem too small to bring about a really decisive improvement.

Living standards in the villages are also being positively influenced by the activities in a variety of ways. This is true, for example, of the health status of the children, which is being promoted directly and indirectly by project operations of various organizations. The fact that the impacts on living standards are visible in the influence matrix but not in the trend analysis is due to the external factors that eclipse any positive effect the project operations may have on living standards in much the same way as the disturbance factors "shortage of rainfall" and "epidemics", preventing them from triggering a change of trend.

Besides having clearly positive impacts, however, the PGRN is causing **land use conflicts** between different population groups. This is due, on the one hand, to the structure of society in the country, in which women are granted fewer rights than men, and land use conflicts between farmers and herders are predestined to occur because of various factors. It is also due, however, to the PGRN's lack of success in counteracting these structures in the project villages – by means of special agreements, for example – so that the project operations may also benefit the disadvantaged groups. Until it succeeds in doing this, the men, with their greater power, will always take the most profitable areas of production for themselves, and the herders will refuse to comply with restrictions on the use of land as long as they themselves do not benefit. Instead of compulsively trying to make the protection of resources attractive to herders, however, they might be persuaded to respect the measures being taken to prevent erosion if the PGRN's present range of activities was joined by others from which they alone benefited. The prospects for success in ensuring compliance with the outcome of negotiations might then improve.

Social Development Profiles and the PGRN's Impact (Development and Impact Profile)

The profiles in Tables 9, 10 and 11 show that during the project period there were significant positive developments in all the villages, and especially Kalé and Ouassala, the two project villages that have been cooperating with the PGRN for some years. However, three factors pose a threat to the positive trend: the deteriorating health status of the children, the increasing tension between farmers and herders and the growing shortage of firewood. The negative trend in the first two of these factors can be deduced directly from the profile line, while the growing shortage of wood is clear from the qualitative evaluation.

Table 9:   Development and impact profile for Kalé

Improvement or impoverishment of livelihoods	92	93	94	95	96	97	Profile line −− +/− ++	Comments by the target groups	Influencing factors[a]
Agricultural yields	5	4	3	4	4	3	OOOO	Yields depend primarily on rainfall. However, they fluctuate less today because of the erosion prevention measures taken by the PGRN.	EF / PGRN
Family incomes	2	3	4	4	4	4	OOOO	The rise in income is due to the PGRN's erosion prevention measures, the horticultural activities and the grain bank, which we have gained with the PGRN's help.	PGRN
Health status of the children	4	4	4	3	1	1	OOOO	The deterioration is due to meningitis epidemics, which, despite the health services, were combated too late or not at all.	EF / OO
Consumer prices of cereals[b]	4	4	4	4	1	5	OOOO	Living standards rise when consumer prices are low, because cereals are bought and not sold.	EF
Access to or exclusion from resources									
Access to firewood	3	3	3	5	5	5	OOOO	Although growing distances have to be covered to reach stocks of firewood, we have a far greater range thanks to the PGRN's donkey carts.	PGRN / EF
Access to drinking water	1	1	1	3	3	3	OOOO	The pump for the well has solved the drinking water problem. We used to have to drink river water, which constantly made us ill.	OO
Access to the market	1	1	1	4	4	4	OOOO	Improvement because of the donkey carts.	PGRN
Access to means of transport	1	1	1	4	4	4	OOOO	Improvement because of the donkey carts.	PGRN
Access to productive land	4	1	2	3	5	5	OOOO	Overuse led to a serious deterioration in 1992, but soil protection measures have since improved matters.	PGRN
Expansion or reduction of knowledge									
Knowledge of sustainable land use	2	3	3	5	5	5	OOOO	Much knowledge was conveyed by the PGRN. Although this has resulted, for example, in our having a better understanding of the herders' interests, we do not tolerate them any more.	PGRN
School enrolment rate	1	1	1	5	5	5	OOOO	Since the construction of the government school enrolment has exceeded 90 %.	OO
Participation in or alienation from rights									
Conflicts[c] between men and women over use of facilities[d]							OOOO	There were no serious conflicts between men and women.	PGRN (?)
Land use conflicts between farmers and herders	3	3	1	1	1	1	OOOO	Following Mali's democratization sanctions against herders for contravening certain laws on resource use were reduced. This also reduced the village authorities' ability to assert themselves. The tree plantations and nature reserves also led to conflicts.	EF / PGRN
Migration[e]	1	4	4	4	4	4	OOOO		EF / PGRN

Key: 5 = very good, 4 = good, 3 = fair, 2 = bad, 1 = very bad

Remarks: a) PGRN = PGRN's influence; OO = influence of another organization's project; EF = external influencing factors. b) The higher the number of points, the lower the prices and the more positive the situation from the target group's point of view. c) The smaller the number of points, the greater the number of conflicts. d) The evaluation was derived from the discussion, but was not undertaken for each year. e) The higher the number of points, the less migration there is and the more favourable the situation from the target group's point of view.

Table 10:   Development and impact profile for Ouassala

Improvement or impoverishment of livelihoods	92	93	94	95	96	97	Profile line (-- +/- ++)	Comments by the target groups	Influencing factors[a]
Agricultural yields	2	5	4	2	3	3	OOOO	Yields are directly dependent on rainfall.	EF
Family incomes	2	3	3	3	4	4	OOOO	While the school was being built, we were employed and paid as building workers. As officials are also paid more regularly today, money is coming into the village.	OO / EF
Health status of the children	3	2	1	1	1	1	OOOO	Children died during the measles and meningitis epidemics. Vaccination campaigns were too late.	OO / EF
Consumer prices of cereals[b]	2	5	4	2	3	2	OOOO	Prices have risen in recent years. This was unfavourable for us, because we had to buy cereals to eat.	EF
Access to or exclusion from resources									
Access to firewood	2	2	1	1	1	1	OOOO	The fact that carts are now available for fetching wood from afar does not make up for the disappearance of the stands of timber.	PGRN / EF
Access to drinking water	4	4	4	4	4	4	OOOO	The four pumps installed for wells in the village in 1990 have solved the drinking water problem.	OO
Access to the market	2	2	2	2	2	2	OOOO	Since we women are not allowed to use the men's donkey carts, access to the market has not changed for us.	PGRN
Access to means of transport	2	2	2	4	4	4	OOOO	The PGRN's donkey carts have greatly improved the situation.	PGRN
Access to productive land	2	2	2	3	4	4	OOOO	The building of stone walls and organic manuring have greatly improved the situation.	PGRN
Expansion or reduction of knowledge									
Knowledge of sustainable land use	2	4	4	4	3	2	OOOO	At first, our knowledge increased significantly. At the moment there is confusion because of the conflicts with the herders.	PGRN
School enrolment rate	3	4	4	5	5	5	OOOO	We have understood that it is better for the children to go to school. Now that we have a school of our own, all the children attend.	OO
Participation in or alienation from rights									
Conflicts[c] between men and women over use of facilities[d]							OOOO	There are conflicts over the donkey carts. As we women are not allowed to use the carts, we are very dissatisfied.	PGRN
Land use conflicts between farmers and herders	4	4	4	4	3	3	OOOO	Conflicts have followed the definition of the routes to be taken by the animals. The herders do not respect them and destroy other areas.	PGRN
Migration[e]	3	3	4	4	4	4	OOOO	Since we have had the donkey carts, the horticultural activities and the grain bank, we have had no reason to leave the village.	PGRN

Key: 5 = very good, 4 = good, 3 = fair, 2 = bad, 1 = very bad

Remarks: a) PGRN = PGRN's influence; OO = influence of other organization's project; EF = external influencing factors. b) The smaller the number of points the higher the prices. c) The smaller the number of points, the greater the conflicts. d) The evaluation was derived from the discussion, but was not undertaken for each year. e) The higher the number of points, the less migration there is and the more favourable the situation.

Table 11: Development and impact profile for Damba

Improvement or impoverishment of livelihoods	94	95	96	97	Profile line -- +/- ++	Comments by the target groups	Influencing factors[a]
Agricultural yields	5	5	5	5	OOOO	Yields are directly dependent on rainfall.	EF
Family incomes	4	4	5	3	OOOO	As the fund-raising for community projects got out of control, our private incomes fell. But this is only true of 1997.	OO / PGRN (?)
Health status of the children	3	3	4	4	OOOO	The health station in Ouassala also enables our children to obtain better health care. Our village has not been affected by epidemics.	OO / EF
Consumer prices of cereals[b]	5	5	4	4	OOOO	Prices have not changed decisively in recent years.	EF
Access to or exclusion from resources							
Access to firewood	2	3	3	3	OOOO	Wood is increasingly difficult to find. But the PGRN's donkey carts generally make the situation easier by increasing the radius of our searches.	PGRN / EF
Access to drinking water	4	4	4	4	OOOO	We got our first pump for the well in 1988. This has solved the drinking water problem.	OO
Access to the market	3	3	4	4	OOOO	The donkey carts from PIDEB for women and the PGRN's have noticeable improved the situation.	OO / PGRN
Access to means of transport	3	4	4	4	OOOO	The PGRN's donkey carts have improved the situation.	PGRN
Access to productive land	2	3	3	3	OOOO	The building of stone walls has improved the situation. Work on filling the compost troughs has only just begun.	PGRN
Expansion or reduction of knowledge							
Knowledge of sustainable land use	3	4	4	4	OOOO	The tree plantations and erosion prevention have taught us a great deal more about land use systems.	PGRN
School enrolment rate	5	5	5	5	OOOO	In the late 1980s two Damba men became teachers. They taught us to go to school. Since then we have sent all our children to school.	EF
Participation in or alienation from rights							
Conflicts[c] between men and women over use of facilities[d]					OOOO	There are conflicts over the use of the donkey carts. Women are not allowed to use the men's carts..	PGRN
Land use conflicts between farmers and herders	2	2	2	2	OOOO	Farmers face growing conflicts because of the planning of land use. Herders do not yet face such conflicts, but do not rule them out in the future. In general, the conflicts worsened even before the PGRN began.	PGRN / EF
Migration[e]	4	4	4	5	OOOO	Our lives have improved in the 1990s, partly because of the PGRN. We will not be leaving.	EF / OO / PGRN

Key: 5 = very good, 4 = good, 3 = fair, 2 = bad, 1 = very bad

Remarks: a) PGRN = PGRN's influence; OO = influence of another organization's project; EF = external influencing factors. b) The smaller the number of points, the higher the prices. c) The smaller the number of points, the greater the conflicts. d) The evaluation was derived from the discussion, but was not undertaken each year. e) The higher the number of points, the less migration there is and the more favourable the situation.

Although the trend in **living standards** is at present mainly dependent on external factors and – where health is concerned – on the support of other organizations, the grain bank assisted by the PGRN has already had a very favourable impact on prospects for survival in all the villages. The PGRN has had its main impact in the natural resource sphere, **access to resources** having become appreciably easier in all the villages. The subsidization of the donkey carts plays a key role in this context.

Knowledge has also improved during the project period, although the very sharp rise in school enrolment rates is due not to the PGRN but to the commitment and growing awareness of the people and the work of other organizations and government services and occurred partly even before the project cycle began. Knowledge of sustainable land use systems has improved significantly as a result of the PGRN's efforts. Although knowledge has improved in Ouassala, there is currently confusion in the village because of the conflicts triggered by land use planning. The people are, however, generally convinced of the usefulness of this knowledge, especially that concerning stone lines.

Where **rights** are concerned, only the PGRN's influence on the potential for conflict between men and women and between farmers and herders was examined. The relationship between farmers and herders has steadily deteriorated or remained poor in all the villages in recent years. The increasing tension between the two socio-professional groups is primarily due to external factors, but because of its work in the natural resource sphere the project provides new sources of friction from which conflicts emerge. The PGRN has yet to find a way of acting as a mediator.

In all the villages **migration**, which is used as an indicator of a minimum of quality of life, has diminished in the 1990s. The main determining factor is the better distribution of rainfall in the 1990s than in the 1980s and 1970s. The PGRN has, however, done a great deal to persuade the target groups to develop an idea of their future lives in the village and to regard staying as not only a desirable but also a realistic option.

CHAPTER 5

Significance of the Operations and Comparison with Observations of the Evaluation Team

The inspection of the project activities that have been undertaken generally produces a positive evaluation, although the impression is that the people tend to overestimate rather than underestimate the current effect of some activities. Their optimistic view is probably due to the fact that, when the influence matrix and the activity list are compiled, the target groups' actual experiences are mixed with the expectations, hopes and interests that they harbour with respect to the operations or cooperation with the project.

The impression of slight overestimation specifically concerns the **"productive operations"**. Although in certain cases these measures may well be very effective,[32] they have hitherto been undertaken de facto by only a small proportion of the farm household systems or over only small areas. Their importance for the whole village is therefore still relatively limited at present and in some cases is confined to the learning and demonstration effect emanating from them. The rate at which the "productive operations" are adapted in the villages has so far been low because of both the considerable willingness to be innovative that such operations require and the extensive labour input and sometimes high cost they entail for the farm household systems.[33] Furthermore, conditions are not suitable on all farms for operations to be undertaken profitably. The "productive operations" are therefore an opportunity for the "better-off" members rather than all members of the target groups to raise their living standards. For this section of the target groups, however, the "productive operations" may also provoke a self-perpetuating multiplier effect in the neighbouring villages.[34]

From the outset, on the other hand, operations that concern the whole village and enable all the villagers to participate have greater importance. This is true of such **community operations** as the grain bank, the school, the health station, wells, etc. In this case the impact of the operations depends mainly on management. As a rule, such operations are not geared to profitability and call for considerable investment, which can never be effected without outside help. This means there is usually no chance of a self-perpetuating multiplier effect. The emphasis is on providing the people with basic social, health and education services, which are essential if human potential is to be tapped for the implementation of the "productive operations".

Between the two extremes are operations that can be undertaken **both by the community and on a private basis**. Specifically, they are, for example, irrigated vegetable and rice growing and the establishment of tree plantations and nature conservation areas. What form the rights of use take in this context depends on the concept in each case. In this case the irrigated vegetable gardens and rice-growing areas probably have greater potential than the impact analysis reveals. However, this is due not to methodological shortcomings but solely to the fact that, as no vegetables had yet been sold, the impact analysis was undertaken six months too soon for an evaluation of the gardens.

Just as there is tension over the "productive operations" between user groups and groups who are unwilling, unable or not allowed to benefit from the operations, there is tension in the region between villages that participate and those not selected as project villages. The logical consequence is that this inequality also leads to **conflicts among the villages**. The project cannot entirely preclude conflicts of this kind, which may be triggered by any positive operation, whatever form it may take. It can only try to provide for compensation, possibly by enabling rights of access to be acquired by people who have not hitherto participated, thus ensuring the fair distribution of opportunities in this respect. On the other hand, although it may be counterproductive in terms of profitability, it should be ensured that villages which are particularly committed and have participated successfully in projects are not repeatedly favoured by donors.

5.4   Conclusions

5.4.1   Effort and Feasibility

After MAPP had been adapted to the specific circumstances of the region, sector and target groups,[35] conducting the test run posed no problems. Using the five instruments took two days per village, which included appropriate breaks and explanations for the target groups. Whether this is a heavy or light workload depends on the number of project villages, on the necessary size of the random sample and on the distance between the various areas of activity. An added factor is the size of the evaluation team. Experience has shown that two people are enough to carry out the impact analysis, provided that they know the location and the relevant local languages of the region and have been trained in the methodology.

The **effort** involved in the evaluation may rise very sharply, however, if the group is divided into subgroups, e.g. groups of men and women. A division of this kind either requires several moderators or doubles the time taken. Although such a division is not always beneficial, it may nonetheless be essential in some cases, where, for example, a genuine discourse does not occur, i.e. the disadvantaged groups do not speak up or are ignored by the majority. This is inconsistent with the goal of a social analysis, in which store is set by uncovering all relevant disadvantages. In the practical example, however, conflicts were uncovered simply because of the heterogeneity of the members of a group participating in the discussion. Another aspect is that evaluation becomes more difficult and more extensive where a division into subgroups is made. Nor can inconsistencies be clarified during the discussion: they may not be revealed until later, during the final analysis of the data.

One difficult substantive task for the moderator during a participatory impact analysis is **to separate the target groups' expectations from their actual experiences**. An added difficulty is that the moderator too may be subject to this phenomenon in the reverse direction. Thus changes perceived by the target groups as constituting major progress may be classified as negligible by the external observer in view of his own, possibly completely different living conditions and a perception of time that is geared to speed. Both perceptions are equally subjective, but the target groups' perception carries greater weight inasmuch as it is they who ultimately have to live with the progress or the reversals. Although the target groups' expectations and interests influence their assessment of the impacts of a project, these positive expectations are also the driving force for the continuation of activities and so are themselves an important positive effect of the project work. It does not therefore seem wise to go too far in questioning the expectations harboured by the target groups in discussions with them. On the other hand, it is appropriate to make sure, by asking for practical examples, for instance, that a close link to reality is maintained. Striking this balance is the moderator's task and calls for experience in the socio-culture concerned and for tact and sensitivity.

The **appraisal of the data** requires relatively little effort and no major calculations. The difficulty with the method lies not in the handling of the documents, which can be prepared in advance for each tool, but rather in interpreting the data correctly and in ensuring the flexibility that the whole analysis requires of the moderator. It is very important to ask about and to note the reasons for specific development. These notes are, after all, crucial if the matrices are to be understood and therefore essential for the whole impact analysis.

MAPP can in principle be carried out by **local project staff**, but not – unless they have previously been trained in the PRA methodology – without their having first attended a practical course in the field. The main aim in such training should be to ensure that the analyses are carried out flexibly rather than mechanically. It must also be understood that a basic requirement if the analyses are to succeed is not to lead the target groups during the group discussions but actually to allow the discussion to continue until consensual results have been achieved or any disputes have clearly been settled. This is difficult in two respects: firstly, because of his personal status and the pressure he is under, the moderator is tempted to manipulate the proceedings, and secondly, the target groups are often willing to be led. It has been found, however, that creative work and a marked willingness to take part in a discussion are immediately apparent when the moderator ceases to feel that he is under pressure. Finding a consensus during a relaxed discussion of this kind was not a problem in any of the villages.

If MAPP is to be successful, it is very important for the target groups to be able to understand the reason for the analysis. During the test run the villagers immediately found the purpose of the analysis plausible. After an introduction lasting approximately half an hour, it was possible to leave the preparation of the matrices to the target groups themselves. It was also obvious that the target groups were well versed in discussion and joined in with great commitment. The identification of divergences and lines of conflict was almost automatic, although the target groups undoubtedly did not single out all the conflicts for discussion.

5.4.2   Validity and Informative Value

The evaluation design is guided by the principle of triangulation, i.e. certain data are collected twice with the aid of different methods or tools. As various data sets overlap, complement or qualify each other at certain points, there is also a chance to correct "mavericks". On the whole, this enhances the **external validity** of the study findings. The external validity of the data is also checked and enhanced through a comparison of data collected by conventional means with data collected by participatory means. The most important tool in this context is direct observation. Idealizations or understatements by the people can be qualified with the aid of one's own observations. A **systematic transect** is therefore always necessary, even for a routine impact analysis.

The simulated "with-and-without comparison" provides indications of the **internal validity** of the data. Accordingly, the project should have had a greater impact in Kalé and Ouassala than in Damba. As the tables show, this is also revealed by the test run, and the differences between the "new" and "old" project villages are visible when the trend and influence matrices are examined.[36] As a further check on the quality of the data the project documents or input and output data from the project's M&E system are consulted. These data are routinely collected by the PGRN's domestic technical personnel. The comparison of the data sets, however, represents not only a check on the data set collected by participatory means but also, conversely, on the M&E data. In the present case the comparison unfortunately reveals that the M&E data need to be reviewed and supplemented before they can be used for further comparisons, let alone monetary calculations.[37]

5.4.3   MAPP's Strengths and Limitations

The method presented enables the social impacts of programmes and projects to be assessed from the target groups' angle with a high degree of plausibility and a differentiated image of the social trends in the project region to be conveyed. The evaluation findings are derived from the evaluation sessions in the project region in completely transparent form and so can be immediately understood or analysed by the reader. As the quantification stage that is undertaken in MAPP to describe the results also permits a comparison of individual survey units, cross-section analyses can be carried out without difficulty.

With MAPP it is also possible to gauge the influence of different programme and project activities on social development and to distinguish the contributions of different organizations without difficulty. MAPP also provides the option of comparing the social developments identified with the project costs with the aid of additional, project-related input and output data. This enables the cost of "village development" to be calculated. As a social impact analysis reveals processes that are constantly evolving as a function of changes in general conditions and project activities, it is advisable to carry out MAPP not only once during the project cycle, but throughout the project at, say, three-year intervals and ex post. Applied ex ante, MAPP can provide useful information on activities lacking or weakly developed social means in a region. If the analysis is made several times in the same villages, the cost on each occasion is far lower, because the considered time axis shorten.

The key question in the assessment of MAPP is how far are the **systematized memories of the target groups** used as an analytical instrument able to produce truthful and inwardly consistent and logical results. As there are no comprehensive studies on the validity of participatory methods, a conclusive answer to this question cannot be given here. From a constructivist and hermeneutic viewpoint, however, it is true to say that the call for absolutely certain knowledge can be qualified by a conception of justifiable knowledge goals. **Validation** then has the task of deciding between competing and falsifying interpretations and of contributing and reviewing arguments in favour of the relative trustworthiness of alternative knowledge goals. Secondly, the change of perspective from conformity with an objective reality in accordance with the classical concept of validity to the constructivist view is also associated with the shift from the observation of reality to its analysis (Kvale 1991, pp. 427 ff.). As the subjective perception of people directly concerned is systematically included in the survey or forms its core element in MAPP, this approach and the lack of viable alternatives provide the only theoretical justification for this way of proceeding (see also the comments in sections 4.2 to 4.4.).

Specific aspects of MAPP will now be discussed, and some of its strengths and areas where further improvement is possible will be indicated:

The effort involved in MAPP depends on the number and heterogeneity of the survey units and so on the size of the random sample needed if valid results are to be produced for the overall project. For large-scale programmes or projects entailing cooperation with several hundred villages it seems appropriate to carry out MAPP in, say, 10 % of the villages selected on the basis of qualitative criteria. Unassisted neighbouring villages must also be included to provide information on synergies and multiplier effects or on any conflicts to which this inequality may give rise.

With the selection of the survey units an attempt can be made to record the overall variance of the project villages, or the criteria can be established on the basis of particularly interesting questions. In the latter case two or more "random sample clusters" as far apart as possible can be formed to permit a comparison of different villages and a classification to be made. The selection criteria otherwise depend on the project variables in the specific region. One of the most important aspects is the analysis of determinants of social development in the various villages. Conceivable variables are project periods of different length, project management (e.g. participatory versus non-participatory cooperation), the social and ethnic differences in the villages and different agri-ecological areas. In projects that have an M&E system villages suitable for evaluation can also be selected with the help of this information. A comparison can be made, for example, between what are found to be "problem villages" and what are found to be "successful villages".

MAPP is suitable for applying in regions where target groups cooperate with one or several poverty-oriented projects or programmes with **short impact chains**. MAPP is more suitable to be applied to the meso than to the micro level because it looks beyond the project level. For the evaluation of projects with indirect poverty links, e.g. at policy level, MAPP is not yet, on the other hand, a suitable method, since it does not include any indicator chains that might enable such repercussions to be recorded. Beside the possibility of scaling up the methodology to make the approach suitable for higher level evaluations (vertical view), a horizontal view can be pronounced also, where a sufficient number of investigations form together a result that is meaningful for the country as a whole.

One of the areas where there is room for further improvement to MAPP is the systematic recording of **general conditions**, which were not therefore taken into account sufficiently during the test run. More statements could be made, for example, on the vulnerability of social development in the villages concerned, on the likelihood of the development achieved being sustained and on the importance of the project in the region as a whole.

By analogy with the DFID's outline concept, MAPP also assumes that the **sustainable management of natural resources** is of necessity associated with ensuring the survival, i.e. **reducing the poverty**, of extremely poor people. However, MAPP differs from the DFID draft in not seeing any fundamental inconsistency between the two objectives. In many geographical regions, and especially in the southern Sahel and in much of the northern Sudan area, the scarcity of resources is already so far advanced that the people are experiencing and have recognized the need for sustainable resource management as being vital now. Consequently, the basic question for extremely poor people is not necessarily whether safeguarding the environment or ensuring survival is more important, but how better to compensate for the economic inconsistency inherent in the short-term view.[38]

MAPP was used here in a **rural context**. How far it is possible and appropriate to apply it to the urban context has not yet been considered. The ODA's four key social factors, however, are by no means restricted to the rural context, especially as the sub-criteria can each be varied. The

PRA methodology has also been used in the urban context on many occasions, although specific difficulties may then arise. Urban target groups may be more difficult to cover than rural groups, for example, and it is likely to take longer to employ some typical PRA tools in the urban context.

Hitherto MAPP has been largely confined to the analysis of physically visible project measures. Measures that are not visible, as in the area of capacity-building, do, however, account for a growing proportion of project measures, and it is therefore equally important for them to be evaluated. The next time MAPP is run in practice the plan is to operationalize these "invisible measures" and to expand the methodology at this point.

MAPP provides points of departure for the processing of seven of the ten problem areas in evaluation to which reference has been made (see section 3.3). Problem areas (6), (9) and (10) are not, however, affected by this, as is explained below. Even though it is essential in MAPP for the partner and, above all, the target groups to participate, the fundamental **problem of the partner's interest** in impact evaluation is not automatically affected (Problem 6). As long as evaluation results may lead to the termination of the donor organization's support, it will be impossible to eliminate this problem. The donor organization's interest in possibly being able to take negative decisions on cooperation nonetheless seems legitimate and necessary.

How to deal with the **time lag** and the **term of impacts** (Problem 9) also remains a big challenge in the further development of MAPP. However, MAPP does enable it to be clearly seen from the annual evaluations in the matrices when the initial impacts of measures were perceived and how long they lasted. No forecasts of the continued stability of the operations are made, on the other hand, but an attempt was made in a follow-up test run in Burkina Faso that deals with this problem.[39] Until now, there is no systematic concept for integrating MAPP results into further project planning. The problem of **implementing evaluation results** (Problem 10) thus can also arise in MAPP's case.

Notes

Chapter 1

1   For the definition and development of evaluation research see also Kraus (1991), pp. 412 ff.

2   Quoted from BMZ (1992a), pp. 9-12. See also Ohe (1982).

3   This reference led to the development of the BMZ's outline concept of *"socio-cultural criteria for development cooperation projects"*, which provided for account to be taken of three defined key socio-cultural factors in all development projects from the planning to the evaluation stage. For further details of this concept see pp. 9-11 and Bliss / Gaesing / Neumann (1997).

4   Schwefel's experimental and quantitative approach requires a large number of cases for "with-and-without comparisons" and also includes so many variables that it would be too expensive for evaluation by organizations.

5   This was again demanded comparatively recently by both governmental and non-governmental organizations at a conference of the German Agency for Technical Co-operation (GTZ) held in Bonn on 25/26 March 1998.

6   In May 1997 the ODA was renamed the Department for International Development (DFID). However, as the concept of key social processes was developed in 1995, the organization will be referred to here by the name it held at the time of the various publications.

Chapter 2

1   In common parlance the education and health sector is regarded as the "social sector".

2   The analytical dimensions of development cooperation can be subdivided into the technical, macroeconomic, microeconomic, institutional, ecological, social and political dimensions.

3   Another field in which overlapping occurs is social psychology, which is not, however, considered in this context.

4   In social economics economic aspects are considered in the societal context, i.e. account is taken of the social structure. Although the existence of social economics in the strict sense is disputed, since it presupposes the existence of pure, non-social economics, the term is used here in a purely pragmatic fashion to distinguish it from socio-cultural factors.

5   For the term "socio-culture" see Ohe (1982), and for the operationalization of this concept see Bliss / Gaesing / Neumann (1997).

6   For the dispute between the cultural theories of evolutionism and cultural relativism and the relevance of this dispute to cooperation on development policy see Bliss / Gaesing / Neumann (1997), pp. 209-229.

7   See Carney (1998), p. 2. The complete concept is to be presented in London in 1998 at the Natural Resources Advisers Conference (NRAC).

8   The ODA offers check lists for the social sectors, infrastructure projects, some "green" sectors (but not natural resource management) and the tourism sector.

9   The sector-related ODA check lists are based on the approach only in substantive terms: they do not make for any further methodological development as regards the way in which data are collected or the way in which findings are presented. Instead, the check list leads to questions being answered in encyclopaedic style, with methodological aspects neglected, and to their being increasingly enriched – as is the case with other matrices of this kind. An approach of this nature makes it difficult to compare analyses and causes greater complexity. As when other concepts are used, there is a lack of transparency, i.e. it is impossible to see on the basis of what data a question has been answered in one way and not another. When it comes to finding a systematic, methodologically unobjectionable approach, then, this is not the solution.

Chapter 3

1   For the concept of sustainability in development cooperation see Stockmann (1997), pp. 2 f.; Stockmann / Kohlmann (1998); Schuster / Pinger (1998), pp. 160 f.

2   The GTZ presented this new self-image in a paper by Klaus (1998) at a conference on 25/26 March 1998. In the ensuing debate on this paper, however, various objections cast doubt on this self-image; see GTZ (1998a), pp. 67 ff.:

1)   Taken to its logical conclusion, such client orientation would mean the donor organization forgoing some development objectives, which would lead to a degree of moral arbitrariness. This elicited the objection that, if what the client wanted was to be taken into account, professional and ethical approach must, of course, be maintained and that the execution of the order must continue to be ensured. Customer satisfaction should be achieved through the usefulness of the outcome.

2)   The client concept presupposes the existence of market mechanisms that indicate fluctuations in acceptance of the quality offered. A free play of market forces does not, however, exist in development cooperation.

3)   A service in development cooperation cannot be compared to a service in the private sector. While the aim of the latter is, for example, to carry out a repair, the aim in development cooperation is to enable those concerned to solve their problems themselves.

3   In governmental evaluation a distinction is made between thematic evaluations, sectoral evaluations, instrument evaluations, institution-related evaluations and individual or project evaluations. A further distinction can be made between cross-

section, series and country evaluations. To illustrate this, a diagram showing the structure of evaluation in German development cooperation can be found in Annex 1.

4   The study has appeared in summer 1999.

5   The most recent version, which appeared in January 1997, is reproduced in the annex.

6   Proposal of 23 June 1997 from Department 310 to the Minister concerning the development of the BMZ's evaluation system, based on a management meeting on 24 April 1997.

7   The World Bank's Operations Evaluation Department (OED) adopts a completely different approach: it publishes all its evaluation reports.

8   Breier (1997), information obtained during an interview.

9   For the monitoring of financial cooperation activities see also KfW (1998a).

10 A project is classified by the KfW as sustainable if it achieves a useful economic life after financial assistance ceases. See KfW (1997b), p. 96.

11 See Erlbeck (1998), pp. 249-263, who explains the DED's performance review procedure. For evaluation by other politically and denominationally independent organizations see, for example, Wiener (1998), pp. 264-269.

12 After not more than six months provisional work plans are updated by the development workers in cooperation with the partner.

13 Being mindful of the personality-forming aspects for development workers is consistent with the DED's self-image.

14 The fact that the Churches are closer to their partners than other organizations is due not only to different convictions but also to different partner structures. In Church cooperation the partners are by no means independent organizations, since their structures were often created and maintained for decades with the Church money of the "donors" and managed by the two sides together. It is thus less risky for a Church organization to be genuinely close to its partners than it may be for non-Church organizations.

15 Another reason for the limited progress made in the development of methods in the past has been the structure of German evaluation. It is largely based on the engagement of consultants who compete with one another and have no interest of their own in the organizations' methodological prescriptions. As they see it, any standardization of evaluations amounts to simplification and is associated with a restriction of their freedoms. A completely transparent approach would, moreover, only exacerbate the competitive situation in which they find themselves.

16 On the initiative of Deutsches Übersee-Institut in Hamburg conferences on progress reviews in development cooperation were held in February 1995 and June 1996, the findings being summarized in Brüne (1998). On 15/16 December 1997 a workshop initiated by the BMZ on the subject of "Methods of observing the impacts of devel-

opment cooperation projects" was held in Berlin. On 25/26 March 1998 a GTZ conference on "Sustained impacts through quality management – a challenge for technical cooperation" took place in Bonn; see GTZ (1998a). The question of impact analysis methods was described as particularly urgent. This picture is rounded off by the study carried out by the HWWA, which is now evaluating progress reviews in Germany. On the international level a workshop of the OECD/DAC Working Party on Aid Evaluation on Approaches and Methods for Evaluation of Development Assistance for Poverty Reduction took place in Edinburgh, 12 - 14 October 1999.

17   To some extent there is still noticeable tension between the two spheres. The main criticisms voiced by the research community stem from the suspicion of partiality in the still dominant internal evaluations undertaken by the organizations and the inadequacy of the methods used. The organizations, on the other hand, regard university evaluations as being unpractical, too complex, time-consuming and costly. They also find fault with university research for being too remote from the partner and criticize the universities' lack of understanding for the legitimacy of political priorities in their decisions. The establishment of *Gesellschaft für Evaluation (DeGEval)* in March 1997, which is represented by a permanent office at the University of Cologne and of which experts from both the research and practical communities are members, would appear, however, to mark the beginning of a change from tension to cooperation. The interinstitutional working groups newly formed to cover various subject areas provide firm foundations for this.

Chapter 4

1   For the following statements see Basaran (1997), pp. 17-20. For more information on research designs see also Rossi / Freeman (1993).

2   Compared to randomized controls, hypothetical and statistical controls in quasi-experimental designs have the disadvantage that, when the test and control units are selected, the evaluator may reduce the initial comparability of the two groups and endanger the internal validity of the outcome of the study as a result of a distorted selection.

3   Where validity is concerned, the question is whether, with the approach adopted, what was to have been measured or what is claimed to have been measured has in fact been measured. Reliability, on the other hand, exists where the same result is achieved in repeated studies of the same phenomenon using the same method. For the terms "validity" and "reliability" and their importance for the quality of empirical studies see also Schnell / Hill / Esser (1995), pp. 141 ff. A critical analysis of the concept of validity and its relevance to research in the social sciences can be found in Kalve (1991), pp. 427 ff.

4   See the discussion of problems encountered in evaluation in Chapter 3.

5   See Patton (1978 and 1987), quoted here from Kraus (1991), p. 413.

6   This also means that they assume there to be a reality.

7   Let us formulate a hypothesis A: "A maintains that reality is a product of my brain." Let us formulate a hypothesis B: "B states that reality is a product of my brain." The fundamental hypothesis of radical constructivism that "reality is a construct of the brain" thus applies precisely when it is true of A and B at the same time, i.e. the principle of relativity generates a third principle, the joint world of imagination, as the central reference variable. It is the medium in which the relationship between "you" and "I" comes true: I exist only through the other person, and he exists only through me; knowing about the other person is my conscience. See Foerster (1992), p. 82.

8   The team forms part of Staff Unit 04, Questions of Principle in the GTZ's Enterprise Development, Eschborn. As a member of this team, Kuby (1997a, b) described the team's views in a paper presented to the World Bank's *Operations Evaluation Department* and during a BMZ symposium.

9   While, for example, the quantity of tree crops harvested would still be relatively easy to determine, on-farm field tests would be needed to establish any increase in yield due to the construction of stone lines. Measuring the longer time it took for a cistern to fill would be even more difficult, however. It would call for models used under realistic laboratory conditions to eliminate the influence of external interference factors (fluctuations in precipitation) and to define the net yield.

10   Thus outcome data do not as a rule cover additional or alternative uses for project operations which were overlooked at the planning stage or are not commensurate with the actual project objective. The increased capacity of the cistern, for example, might also be used by the target group to irrigate vegetable fields around the waterhole. Such changes of use occur regularly and may well constitute an improvement on the original planning. An advance calculation based on planned use would thus produce an irrelevant or incorrect result in this case.

11   A further difficulty for the analysis is that not only are the changes in general conditions additional to the changes caused by project operations, but that synergies occur between the two kinds of change.

12   In 1992 the International Fund for Agricultural Development (IFAD) published a study on the participatory element of evaluations specifically in the rural development sector. The following comments on participatory evaluation methods are based on this study.

13   For further conceptual classification and definition see, for example, Kittel (1997), pp. 28 ff.

14   See GTZ / gate (1996); World Bank (no year); World Bank (1994; 1995b); IFAD (1992); Ham et al. (1995); Narayan (1993). The OED and USAID both have journals devoted entirely to evaluation: OEC-Précis, e.g. No 3, and USAID: Tips. Performance Monitoring and Evaluation, e.g. No 183.

15   For a further definition of this concept see section 3.12.

16   This view is taken, for example, by Stockmann (1997).

17   These criteria were, for example, declining dependence on the landowner, less
      dependence on child labour in the rainy period, better seasonal distribution of income,
      a more varied diet, a better supply of clothing and better hygienic conditions. See
      World Bank (no year), p. 12.

18   For example, qualitative educational research, family research, evaluation research,
      organizational research, market research, media research, etc. See Mayring (1990),
      pp. 3 ff.

19   See Klingebiel (1992), pp. 4 ff. and, for the formation of indicators in poverty impact
      monitoring, Carvalho / White (1994).

20   In practical evaluation, however, no distinction is made between the terms "indicator"
      and "criterion".

21   One example is the World Bank's *Zambia Poverty Assessment* (1994).

22   In principle, the subcriteria may also be established by the target group from the
      outset. In this case preference was given to the prior selection for all the villages be-
      ing made by the project staff in order to ensure comparability among the villages.

23   See Schnell / Hill / Esser (1995); Flick et al. (1991); Valadez / Bamberger (1994),
      Chapters 9 and 10; Friedrichs (1985), Chapter 5 on methods, pp. 189-376.

24   The following comments are largely based on Schönhuth / Kievelitz (1993).

25   There are also a number of other participatory approaches, of which only a few
      random examples will be given here. *Agroeconomics Analysis (AEA)* takes account
      of and records the networking of ecological, economic and socio-economic processes;
      see Conway / Pretty / McCracken (1987). *Beneficiary Assessment (BA)* focuses par-
      ticularly on groups who are difficult to reach and have no voice and obtains feedback
      on project operations; see Salmen (1992). *Participatory Action Research (PAR)* is
      based on action research and can be regarded as a strategy for creating awareness and
      mobilization. Change, i.e. the identification and settlement of conflicts, is an integral
      part of the method; see Huizer (1989).

26   See Schönhuth / Kievelitz (1993), pp. 56 ff. In 1994 the World Bank published a
      collection of participatory survey tools which, though developed for use in the "water
      and drinking water" sector, can also be used in other sectors. The manual, which is
      accompanied by a tool kit, presents numerous tools, some of which are suitable for
      inquiries into social contents. They are mentioned here even though they are not ex-
      plicitly attributed to the PRA tools. See also Narayan (1993).

27   For gender-related techniques and training for the evaluation process see the World
      Bank's Development Tool Kit (1994).

Chapter 5

1   For further details see, for example, Vester / Hesler (1980).

2   There are plans for MAPP to be used and tested again in 1999 in a resource management project implemented by the Agriculture Ministry in Burkina Faso (PATE-CORE). The project is being supported and co-financed by the GTZ and KfW. It will provide a further opportunity for evaluations to be conducted in a wide range of villages.

3   See the discussion of the idea of solidarity and efficiency in section 3.2.4.

4   It would be absurd, for example, to consider whether easier access to resources is more important than acquiring know-how. All four key social processes are equally important for maintaining the social system.

5   A comparison of the social impacts of a project with M&E data nevertheless seems interesting provided that the data are treated with due caution. To this end, the PGRN M&E data were compared with the data collected by the evaluation team. A comparison of the data sets, however, raised so many questions that the site would have to be visited again before further evaluation along these lines could be contemplated.

6   See World Bank (1995c)): Evaluation à mi-parcours de Décembre 1995 – Aide-mémoire –, PGRN, Bamako 1995.

7   Further information on the PGRN can be found, for example, in: (1) Ministère du Développement Rural et de l'Environnement/ida/gtz (1995): Fiche de Présentation du Projet de Gestion des Ressources Naturelles (PGRN), Mali. (2) GTZ (1997): Projektkurzbeschreibung: Projet de Gestion des Ressources Naturelles (PGRN), Mali. (3) Ministère du Développement Rural et de l'Environnement/ida/gtz (1994): Elaboration d'un Plan d'Aménagement/Plan de Gestion des Terroirs – Manuel de Planification, PGRN, Bamako, Mali.

8   Grios have the task of conveying news, telling stories and acting as spokesmen. During one of these evaluation meetings, for example, a grio "translated" all the speeches by the village head into a form that all the members of the evaluation group would find easier to understand (story form).

9   The literacy rate in Ouassala is far higher than in Kalé, where it is higher than in Damba. This grading also corresponds to the proximity of these villages to Bafoulabé.

10   In some cases the matrices for Damba are the best prepared because this village was visited last and the method was therefore farthest advanced by that time. The development and impact profiles, which represent, as it were, the synthesis of the various instruments, are shown for all the villages in the main part of the study.

11   The career lines of the other villages are shown in Figures A1 and A2. In the first village a period of 28 years was chosen. It was found, however, that the group was unable to remember so far back. The participants did not, on the other hand, want to combine several years in the discussion. This is probably due to the fact that annual

precipitation is the most important minimum factor – see other comments – and precipitation varies widely from one year to another.

12 The reason given for this, however, was slightly sobering: for the villagers democracy meant the freedom to cut wood without being punished.

13 A bush fire destroyed a large proportion of the harvest in 1987. To add to this disastrous loss, the village had to pay a fine to the authorities because lighting bush fires was forbidden.

14 Tables relating to the other two villages can be found in the annex. Experience showed that it is appropriate and there is time for a longer period than seven years to be examined. The periods for the following villages were therefore extended.

15 As the PIDEB in particular was active in Damba before the PGRN, the difference is not so pronounced as might originally have been expected.

16 Where access to firewood is concerned, however, the gain is questionable, since it can be ascribed not to an improved supply of wood but to the wider radius over which wood can be collected thanks to the donkey carts and will therefore be transitory. This situation has now occurred in Ouassala. Access to firewood there has already worsened despite new donkey carts.

17 In Ouassala, however, growing conflicts with the herders are preventing new know-how from being put to use.

18 This may be exceptional among the Sahel countries.

19 As the health station was set up not with the PGRN's help but by another organization, more detailed information is not currently available.

20 For more precise information on this see Ministère du Développement et de l'Environnement/ida/GTZ: Synthèse de l'Atelier de Restitution des Résultats du Praset dans une Zone d'Intervention du PGRN, Yelimane, 28-30 May 1997, Mali.

21 It was found that joint evaluation with all the relevant social groups was particularly good at revealing areas of friction and conflicts in the villages. This shows that separate meetings are far from always bound to produce more differentiated findings. Further research on this is planned.

22 A decline in migration was rated positively by the target groups and was awarded ever higher numbers of points. This is by no means to be expected, since migration might also be rated positively by the rural population because migrants usually send money to the village and so provide development aid for those left behind. Leaving the village may also have positive associations in that it is evidence of modernity and cosmopolitan attitudes. Such thinking was clearly not decisive in the target groups' evaluation: social cohesion and thus the maintenance of the system of social safeguards were given a higher rating.

23 In Kalé and Ouassala an attempt was initially made to portray this information with the aid of VENN diagrams. This was not successful, and ranking was instead applied,

but it similarly lacked informative value. It was not until Damba that the information was collected with a simple chart filled in jointly on the basis of the proven scale of one to five. This approach posed no difficulties for the target groups and also had the largest information content. The activity lists for Kalé and Ouassala thus had to be composed with the fragmentary information obtained from the VENN diagram and the ranking and converted into table form. The information on Kalé and Ouassala is therefore not complete.

24   This is not evident in Damba's case, because its inhabitants use the schools and health stations of the other villages.

25   The PGRN subsidizes 50% of the cost of the donkey carts provided that there is a commitment to undertake erosion prevention measures. The purchaser must always contribute FCFA 75,000 of the cost of a donkey cart.

26   The fattening of sheep is an exception because it is a task performed by the women. It has not been very successful, however, since its profitability is doubtful owing to the high purchase price of sheep.

27   The irrigation systems in Kalé and Ouassala had just been completed. In Ouassala mistakes were made during the curing of the cement (it was not poured and was crumbly). The gardens are of an imposing size and give the impression of being very well looked after. It is not clear, however, how the produce is to be marketed unless the women have donkey carts. Output will undoubtedly far exceed local requirements. For many families the income potential seems considerable if the marketing problem can be solved. The tree plantations are still very young and seem rather small when compared to the growing demand for firewood, the area under trees in each village being not more than half to one hectare.

28   The information provided by the target groups and the data from the M&E system are inconsistent here. The M&E system indicates a significant financial burden on the village population, although the villagers themselves are unable to confirm this. These data need to be reviewed by the PGRN project staff.

29   The donkey cart is the only means of transport in the villages, and greater mobility is one of the most important development factors. Transport is needed not only for active erosion prevention through the construction of stone lines but also for access to more distant health stations and to the market, making it possible to rise above sub-sistence level and take income-generating measures. The availability of a donkey cart also facilitates access to wood and, often enough, to water.

30   Evidently, PIDEB once made a donkey cart available for the women in Damba. This project failed because the women were unable to use the cart properly. Traditionally, leading donkeys and oxen is the preserve of the men and boys. The first step should be to clarify with the women what rules on the use of this means of transport might be laid down.

31   Wood used to be carried by the women on their heads; the men now use the carts to transport it.

32   This is true of the composting facilities and stone lines, since they increase productiv-
     ity per unit area by 30 - 60%, as on-farm field tests undertaken by the PGRN have
     shown.

33   It costs FCFA 75,000 (about US $ 118) to acquire a subsidized donkey cart, a sum
     that by no means all families can afford.

34   Filling composting troughs, for example, calls for a certain number of animals, which
     few farming units possess.

35   When the method is adapted, it must be ensured that the target groups are already
     familiar with the PRA methods. If they are not, more time may need to be taken over
     explanations in the village. It may also be important for the rating scales to be adapted
     to the habits of the target groups. Although in our specific case the target groups were
     able to use the one-to-five points system very satisfactorily, they were confused by
     zero and by the plus and minus signs. The various needs of the target groups were
     taken into account, and recoding was undertaken subsequently.

36   The differences would be even clearer if PIDEB had had no influence, but it has been
     assisting certain projects in Damba for over ten years.

37   Local personnel also need training in the collection and entry of M&E data. The
     present data set lacks explanations for data that depart more significantly from what
     was expected. This might result in their being considered faulty. Conversion factors,
     e.g. the monetarization of work, should be mentioned and explained. The opportunity
     costs hitherto applied for work in the villages seem far too high at US $ 3.23/hr. The
     establishment of initial or planning data should also be explained. Significant depar-
     tures from plans require justification. Data not collected (missing values) should be
     marked as such rather than with "0", which may lead to incorrect calculations. Oper-
     ating costs should also be deducted from investment costs. The nature of the costs
     should always be identified.

38   For this aspect see also the studies undertaken by Neubert (1998) in extremely poor
     regions of Chad.

39   The results of this study will be published by early 2000.

Bibliography

Adam, E. (1998): Analyse und Bewertung der Erfolgskontrolle in der Friedrich-Ebert-Stiftung (FES). Schreiben an das HWWA vom 5.2.1998. Friedrich-Ebert-Stiftung, Projektgruppe Entwicklungspolitik, Bonn

Asian Development Bank (ADB) (1993): *Guidelines for Incorporation of Social Dimensions in Bank Operations*, Manila

— (1994): *Handbook for Incorporation of Social Dimensions in Projects*, Manila

Basaran, T. (1997): Evaluierung von Maßnahmen zur Förderung von Demokratie und Menschenrechten. Ansätze - Methoden - Ergebnisse, GDI, Berlin (unpublished manuscript)

Belshaw, D. (1981): "A Theoretical Framework for Data-economising Appraisal Procedures with Applications for Rural Development Planning", in: *IDS Bulletin*, Vol. 12, No. 4, pp. 12-22

Bliss, F. / K. Gaesing / S. Neumann (1997): *Operationalisierung der sozio-kulturellen Schlüsselfaktoren. Empfehlungen für die deutsche staatliche Entwicklungszusammenarbeit*, Forschungsauftrag des BMZ, Bonn

Borrmann A., et al. (1998): Analyse und Bewertung der Erfolgskontrolle in der deutschen Entwicklungszusammenarbeit. Kurzbeschreibung der Studie, HWWA (Institut für Wirtschaftsforschung), Hamburg (unpublished manuscript)

Brandt, H. (1982): *Projektplanung in der kleinbäuerlichen Produktion*, GDI, Berlin

Breier, H. (1998a): Neukonzeption des Systems der EZ-Erfolgskontrolle. Vortrag auf der Fachtagung der GTZ: "Nachhaltige Wirkungen durch Qualitätsmanagement - eine Herausforderung für die TZ", 25/26 March 1998, Bonn

— (1998b): "Erfolgskontrolle in der Entwicklungszusammenarbeit", in: *E+Z*, Vol. 39, No. 5/6, pp. 128 ff.

Brüne, S. (ed.) (1998): *Erfolgskontrolle in der entwicklungspolitischen Zusammenarbeit*, Schriften des Deutschen Übersee-Institutes, No. 39, Hamburg

Bryk, A. (1983): *Stakeholder - Base Evaluation*, San Francisco

Bundesministerium für wirtschaftliche Zusammenarbeit und Entwicklung (BMZ) (1988): *Förderung von Frauen in Entwicklungsländern*, Bonn

— (1990a): Querschnittsanalyse Sozio-kulturelle Faktoren, Referat 201, Bonn

— (1990b): "Armutsbekämpfung durch Hilfe zur Selbsthilfe - Selbsthilfebewegungen als Partner der Entwicklungszusammenarbeit", in: *BMZ-aktuell*, No. 6

— (1992a): Sozio-kulturelle Kriterien für Vorhaben der Entwicklungszusammenarbeit, Rahmenkonzept, Bonn

— (1992b): "Sozio-kulturelle Fragen in der Entwicklungspolitik", in: *Entwicklungspolitik - Materialien*, No. 83, Bonn

— (1992c): "Hauptelemente der Armutsbekämpfung", in: *BMZ-aktuell*, No. 20

— (1995): "Sektorübergreifendes Zielgruppenkonzept - Die beteiligten Menschen in der Entwicklungszusammenarbeit", in: *BMZ-aktuell*, No. 56

Carney, D. (1998): Implementing the Sustainable Rural Livelihoods Approach. Paper presented at the 14th Annual Meeting between the European Fisheries Co-operation Advisors and the Commission, 14/15 September 1998, Göteborg

Carruthers, L. / R. Chambers (1981): Rapid Appraisal for Rural Development, in: *Agricultural Administration*, Vol. 8, No. 6, pp. 407-422

Carvalho, S. / H. White (1994): Indicators for Monitoring Poverty Reduction, World Bank Discussion Papers, No. 254, World Bank, Washington

Cernea, M. (1985): *Putting People First. Sociological Variables in Rural Development*, World Bank/IBRD, Washington

Chambers, R. (1981): *Rapid Rural Appraisal: Rationale and Repertoire*, IDS Discussion Papers, No. 155, Sussex

— (1992): *Rural Appraisal: Rapid, Relaxed and Participatory*, IDS Discussion Papers, No. 311, Sussex

— (1994): "Participatory Rural Appraisal (PRA): Challenges, Potential and Paradigm", in: *World Development*, Vol. 22, No. 10, pp. 1437-1454

Conway, G.R. / J.N. Pretty / J.A. McCracken (1987): *An Introduction to Agro-ecosystem Analysis. Sustainable Agriculture Programme*, IIED, London

Deutsche Bundesregierung (1994): Deutsche Entwicklungspolitik: Memorandum der Bundesregierung zur DAC-Jahresprüfung 1994/95, 28 November 1994, Bonn

Deutsche Gesellschaft für Technische Zusammenarbeit (GTZ) (no year): Projektbeschreibung PGRN, Eschborn

— (1991): PFK - Leitfaden für die Projektfortschrittskontrolle, Gruppe 1002, Qualitätssicherung, GTZ-Form 23-15-6, Eschborn

— (1992): *Monitoring und Evaluierung in Projekten der Technischen Zusammenarbeit*, Schriftenreihe der GTZ, No. 229, Eschborn

— (1996): Erreicht die Technische Zusammenarbeit ihre gesetzten Ziele? Projektergebnisse der GTZ und ihrer Partner: Zweite Querschnittsanalyse, Eschborn

— (1997a): Monitoring und Evaluierung. Eine Orientierung für laufende Vorhaben in der technischen Zusammenarbeit, Stabstelle 04, Eschborn (draft)

— (1997b): Projektkurzbeschreibung: Projet de Gestion des Ressources Naturelles (PGRN), Bamako/Mali

— (1998a): Nachhaltige Wirkungen durch Qualitätsmanagement - Eine Herausforderung für die Technische Zusammenarbeit. GTZ-Fachtagung in Bonn, 25/26 March 1998, Dokumentation der Ergebnisse, Stabstelle 04, Team "Interne Evaluierung", Eschborn

— (1998b): Monitoring im Projekt. Eine Orientierung für Vorhaben in der Technischen Zusammenarbeit, Stabstelle 04, Eschborn

Deutscher Entwicklungsdienst (DED) (1997): Verbesserung des DED-Beitrags durch Stärkung der Außenstruktur, Rundschreiben, No. 29/97, Berlin

— (1998a): Arbeitsplätze in Projekten und Programmen, Rundschreiben, No. 19/98, Berlin

— (1998b): Die Stimmen der Partner. Partnerinterviews anläßlich der Gesamtkonferenz 1997 zum Thema: "DED - Wohin?". Standortbestimmung und Zukunftsfähigkeit des Deutschen Entwicklungsdienstes, Berlin

Development Assistance Committee (DAC) (1992): *Development Assistance Manual. DAC Principles for Effective Aid*, OECD, Paris

Dittmar, M. / P. Neuhoff (1971): Sozio-ökonomische Probleme der Entwicklungsländer und Kapitalhilfeprojekte, Veröffentlichungen aus dem Arbeitsbereich der Kreditanstalt für Wiederaufbau, No. 9, Frankfurt

Dolzer, H., et al. (1998): *Wirkungen und Nebenwirkungen. Ein Beitrag von Misereor zur Diskussion über Wirkungsverständnis und Wirkungserfassung in der Entwicklungszusammenarbeit*, Aachen

Dütting, M., et al. (1992): *Evaluierung in der kirchlichen Entwicklungsarbeit. Ein Arbeitsbuch für Partnerorganisationen und Hilfswerke*, AGKED und MISEREOR, Aachen

Erlbeck, R. (1998): "Wirkungsbeobachtung in der Personellen Zusammenarbeit (PZ)", in: S. Brüne (ed.), *Erfolgskontrolle in der entwicklungspolitischen Zusammenarbeit*, Schriften des Deutschen Übersee-Instituts, No. 39, Hamburg

Finck, A. (1992): *Dünger und Düngung. Grundlagen und Anleitung zur Düngung der Kulturpflanzen*, Weinheim

Flick, U., et al. (eds) (1991): *Handbuch der Qualitativen Sozialforschung*, Munich

Foerster, H. v. (1992): "Entdecken oder Erfinden", in: H. von Foerster (ed.), *Einführung in den Konstruktivismus*, Munich

Friedrichs, J. (1985): *Methoden empirischer Sozialforschung*, 13th edition, Opladen

Gsänger, H. / T. Voipio (1997): Who Benefits from Aid? Poverty Orientation of European Donors, Country Study Nepal, GDI, Berlin / IDS, Helsinki (Partial Draft)

Guba, E. / S. Lincoln (1989): *Fourth Generation Evaluation*, London

Ham, L., et al. (eds) (1995): *A Draft Guide to Evaluating Sustainable Livelihood Outcomes of Participatory Projects*, International Institute for Sustainable Development (IISD), Winnipeg/Manitoba

Hillebrand, W. / D. Messner / J. Meyer-Stamer (1993): *Stärkung technologischer Kompetenz in Entwicklungsländern*, GDI, Berlin

House, E. R. (1980): *Evaluation with Validity*, Beverly Hills

Huizer, G. (1989): *Action Research and People's Participation. An introduction and some case studies*, Nijmegen

International Fund for Agricultural Development (IFAD) (1992): Participatory Evaluation of Rural Development Projects. Special Studies: Monitoring and Evaluation Division, Report No. 0385

Kamla, B. (1985): Participatory Evaluation: Are we on the Right Track? Report of Secunderabad Workshop on Participatory Self-Evaluation. Ideas and Action, FAO, Freedom from Hunger Campaign, Rome

Kasch, V. (1997): Protokoll eines Workshops zur Projektevaluierung vom 13.-15.6.1997 in Bonn, Evangelische Zentralstelle für Entwicklungshilfe (EZE), Bonn

Klingebiel, S. (1992): Entwicklungsindikatoren in der politischen und wissenschaftlichen Diskussion, INEF Report, Institut für Entwicklung und Frieden der Universität-GH-Duisburg zur wissenschaftlichen Begleitung der Stiftung Entwicklung und Frieden, No. 2/1992, Universität Duisburg

Kingsbury, D. S. / E. P. Brown / P. Poukouta (1995): Alternative Survey Methodologies for Monitoring and Analyzing Poverty in Sub-Saharan Africa. A Study for the SPA Working Group on Poverty and Social Policy, DAI (Development Alternatives Inc.), Maryland

Kittel, S. (1997): Partizipative Erhebungsmethoden in der Entwicklungszusammenarbeit und ihr Einsatz bei der Evaluierung kreditvergebender NGOs, Diplomarbeit, Freie Universität Berlin, FB Wirtschaftswissenschaften (FB 10) and Institut für Bank- und Finanzwirtschaft, Berlin

Klaus, P. (1998): "Qualität und Qualitätsmanagement". Vortrag auf der Fachtagung der GTZ: "Nachhaltige Wirkungen durch Qualitätsmanagement - eine Herausforderung für die TZ", 25/26 March 1998, Bonn

Kohlmann, U. (1998): information provided orally, Bonn

Konrad-Adenauer-Stiftung e.V. (KAS) (1994): *Wirkungskontrolle von Entwicklungsprojekten. Arbeitsbereich Internationale Zusammenarbeit*, Sankt Augustin

Kraus, W. (1991): "Qualitative Evaluationsforschung", in: U. Flick et al. (ed.), *Handbuch qualitative Sozialforschung*, Munich, pp. 421-415

Kreditanstalt für Wiederaufbau (KfW) (1992): Sozio-kulturelle Fragestellungen bei Vorhaben der Finanziellen Zusammenarbeit. Arbeitshilfen, Materialien, Diskussionsbeiträge, No. 3, Auslandssekretariat, 2nd edition, Frankfurt/M.

— (1997a): *Zusammenarbeit mit Entwicklungsländern. Erläuterungen zum Verfahren der Finanziellen Zusammenarbeit der Bundesrepublik Deutschland*, Frankfurt/M.

— (1997b): Ergebnisse der Finanziellen Zusammenarbeit. Vierter Auswertungsbericht über geförderte Vorhaben in Entwicklungsländern, Frankfurt/M.

— (1998a): Projektmonitoring in der FZ. Arbeitshilfen, Materialien, Diskussionsbeiträge, No. 2, Auslandssekretariat, veränderter Nachdruck, Frankfurt/M.

— (1998b): Inhalte und Methoden der Zielgruppenanalyse bei Vorhaben der Finanziellen Zusammenarbeit. Arbeitshilfen, Materialien, Diskussionsbeiträge, Frankfurt/M.

Kuby, T. (1997a): Performance Evaluation of Development Aid, Auszüge aus einem Vortrag bei der OED, World Bank, Washington

— (1997b): Praxis und Reform des Evaluierungssystems der Weltbank auf dem Symposium: "Methoden der Wirkungsbeobachtung in der Evaluierungspraxis von Projekten der entwicklungspolitischen Zusammenarbeit", 15/16 December 1997, Berlin

Kumar, K. (ed.) (1996a): *Rapid Appraisal Methods*, World Bank Regional and Sectoral Studies, World Bank, Washington

— (1996b): "An Overview of Rapid Appraisal Methods in Development Settings", in: K. Kumar, (ed.), *Rapid Appraisal Methods*, World Bank Regional and Sectoral Studies, World Bank, Washington

Kvale, S. (1991): "Validierung: Von der Beobachtung zu Kommunikation und Handeln", in: U. Flick et al. (eds), *Handbuch der Qualitativen Sozialforschung*, Munich, pp. 427-431

Lachenmann, G. (1988): *Sozio-kulturelle Bedingungen und Wirkungen in der Entwicklungszusammenarbeit*, GDI, Berlin

Mayring, P. (1990): *Einführung in die qualitative Sozialforschung. Eine Anleitung zu qualitativem Denken*, Munich

McNamara, R. S. (1973): Ansprache an die Gouverneure in Nairobi am 24.9.1973, in: R.S. McNamara (ed.), *Die Jahrhundertaufgabe - Entwicklung der Dritten Welt*, Stuttgart, pp. 156-197

Meentzen, A. (1998): Leitfaden für externe Beratungseinsätze für die Heinrich-Böll-Stiftung, Berlin (unpublished manuscript)

Ministère du Développement Rural et L'Environnement / ida / GTZ (1994): Elaboration d'un Plan d'Aménagement / Plan de Gestion des Terroirs. Manuel de Planification, PGRN, Bamako/Mali

— (1995): Fiche de Présentation du Projet de Gestion des Ressources Naturelles, PGRN, Bamako/Mali

— (1997): Synthèse de l'Atelier de Restitution des Résultats du Praset dans une Zone d'Intervention du PGRN, Yelimane, 28-30 May 1997, Mali

Mohs, R. (1997): Praxis der Wirkungsbeobachtung in der Entwicklungszusammenarbeit der Europäischen Union. Vortrag anläßlich des Symposiums "Methoden der Wirkungsbeobachtung in der Evaluierungspraxis von Projekten in der entwicklungspolitischen Zusammenarbeit", 15/16 December 1997, Berlin

Müller, O. (1996): "Das Gehirn im Tank", in: *Die ZEIT*, No. 32, 2 August 1996

Musto, S. (1972): *Evaluierung sozialer Entwicklungsprojekte*, GDI, Berlin

Mutter, T. (1995): "Kritische Rückfragen an den Methodenboom in der Entwicklungspolitik", in: *Peripherie*, No. 57/58, pp. 165-175

— (1998): "Aussagefähigere Erfolgskontrolle durch verbesserte Methoden?", in: S. Brüne (ed.), *Erfolgskontrolle in der entwicklungspolitischen Zusammenarbeit*, Schriften des Deutschen Übersee-Instituts, No. 39, Hamburg, pp.132-148

Narayan, D. (1993): Participatory Evaluation. Tools for Managing in Water and Sanitation, Technical Paper, No. 207, World Bank, Washington

Narayan, D. / L. Srinivasan (eds) (1994): Participatory Development Tool Kit. Training Materials for Agencies and Communities, Washington

National Council for Applied Economics Research (NCAER) (1993): *Comparative Study of Sample Surveys and Participatory Rural Appraisal Methods*, New Delhi

Neubert, S. (1998): "Armut und Ansatzpunkte zur Selbsthilfe in der Baumwollregion des Tschad. Eine ökonomische Analyse kleinbäuerlicher Betriebs-Haushalts-Systeme", in: *Sozialökonomische Schriften zur Ruralen Entwicklung*, Vol. 119, Kiel, Berlin, Göttingen

Ohe, W. v.d., et al. (1982): Die Bedeutung sozio-kultureller Faktoren in der Entwicklungstheorie und -praxis. Forschungsbericht des BMZ, Nr. 29, in: Sozio-kulturelle Fragen in der Entwicklungspolitik, Entwicklungspolitik - Materialien, No. 83, Bonn, pp. 10 f.

Operation Evaluation Department (OED) / Weltbank (1996): Performance Monitoring Indicators. A handbook for Task Managers, http://www.worldbank. org/html/opr/pmi/maintxt.html, last updated 30 August 1996

Overseas Development Administration (ODA) (1995): *A Guide to Social Analysis for Projects in Developing Countries*, HMSO, London

Patton, M. Q. (1972): *Utilization-Focused Evaluation*, Beverly Hills

Preuss, H.-J. von / V. Steigerwald (1996): Wirkungsbeobachtung in der GTZ. Von der Projektfortschrittskontrolle zu Qualitätsmanagement. Beitrag der GTZ zur Konferenz des Deutschen Übersee-Instituts "Erfolgskontrolle in der entwicklungspolitischen Zusammenarbeit" in Hamburg, 10/11 July 1996, Stabstelle 04, Grundsatzfragen der Unternehmensentwicklung, Eschborn

Rossi, P. H. / H. E. Freeman (1993): *Evaluation. A Systematic Approach*, 5th edition, London

Roth, G. (1994): *Das Gehirn und seine Wirklichkeit*, Frankfurt/M.

Salmen, L. F. (1987): Listen to the People. Participant - Observer - Evaluation of Development Projects, World Bank (IBRD), New York etc.

— (1992): Beneficiary Assessment. An Approach Described, Working Paper, No. 1, Technical Department, Africa Region, Washington

Schneider, H. / M.-H. Libercier (eds) (1995): in: P. Rossi / H.E. Freeman / G. Hofmann (ed.) (1990), Programm-Evaluation. Einführung in die Methoden angewandter Sozialforschung, Stuttgart

Schnell, R. / P.B. Hill / E. Esser (eds) (1995): *Methoden der empirischen Sozialforschung*, Munich

Schönhuth, M. / U. Kievelitz (1993): *Partizipative Erhebungs- und Planungsmethoden in der Entwicklungszusammenarbeit*, Schriftenreihe der Deutschen Gesellschaft für Technische Zusammenarbeit (GTZ), No. 231, Eschborn

Schuster, W. / W. Pinger (1998): "Nachhaltige Wirksamkeit in der EZ. Ein gemeinsamer Antrag der Fraktionen im Bundestag", in: *E+Z*, Vol. 39, No. 7, pp. 160 f.

Schwefel, D. (1978): *Basic Needs - Planning and Evaluation*, GDI, Berlin

Steigerwald, V. (1998): "Das Qualitätsmanagement der GTZ". Vortrag auf der Fachtagung der GTZ: "Nachhaltige Wirkungen durch Qualitätsmanagement - eine Herausforderung für die TZ" am 25./26.3.1998, Bonn

Stockmann, R. (1996a): "Defizite der Wirkungsbeobachtung", in: *E+Z*, Vol. 37, No. 8

— (1996b): *Die Wirksamkeit der Entwicklungshilfe. Eine Evaluation der Nachhaltigkeit von Programmen und Projekten*, Opladen

— (1997): Methoden der Nachhaltigkeitsanalyse: Zur Konzeption und praktischen Umsetzung. Vortrag anläßlich des Symposiums "Methoden der Wirkungsbeobachtung in der Evaluierungspraxis von Projekten in der entwicklungspolitischen Zusammenarbeit", 15/16 December 1997, Berlin

Stockmann, R. / U. Kohlmann (1998): Nachhaltigkeit und entwicklungsfördernde Wirkungen. Versuch einer Begriffsbestimmung. Vortrag auf der Fachtagung der GTZ: "Nachhaltige Wirkungen durch Qualitätsmanagement - eine Herausforderung für die TZ" am 25./26.3.1998, Bonn

United Nations Development Programme (UNDP) (1997): *Human Development Report*, New York, Oxford

Uphoff, N. (1985): "Fitting Projects to People", in: M. Cernea (ed.), *Putting People First. Sociological Variables in Rural Development*, World Bank/IBRD, Washington, pp. 359-395

Valadez, J. / M. Bamberger (1994): *Monitoring and Evaluating Social Programs in Developing Countries. A Handbook for Policy Makers, Managers and Researchers*, Washington

Vester, F. / A. v. Hesler (1980): *Sensitivitätsmodell*, Frankfurt/M.

World Bank (no year): Combining the Quantitative and Qualitative Approaches to Poverty Measurement and Analysis. The Practice and the Potential, in: S. Carvalho / H. White, World Bank Technical Paper No. 266, Washington

— (1993): Expanding OED's Program of Impact Evaluations. Proposed Principles and Procedures. Working Paper prepared by the interim Group of the World Bank, Washington

— (1994a): *Social Indicators of Development 1994*, Washington

— (1994b): Zambia Poverty Assessment (in five volumes), Report No. 12985-ZA, Human Resources Division, 10 November 1994, Washington

— (1995a): Social Assessment. Environmental Department Dissemination Papers, No. 36, September, Washington

— (1995b): *The World Bank Participation Sourcebook*, Washington

— (1995c): Evaluation à mi-parcours de Décembre 1995, Aide-mémoire, PGRN, Bamako

— (1996): Social Development and Results on the Ground. Task Group Report, 16 September, Washington (unpublished manuscript)

Wiener, M. (1998): "Das Evaluierungsinstrumentarium der Deutschen Welthungerhilfe", in: S. Brüne (ed.), *Erfolgskontrolle in der entwicklungspolitischen Zusammenarbeit*, Schriften des Deutschen Übersee-Instituts, No. 39, Hamburg

ANNEX

Annex 1

Progress review in development cooperation

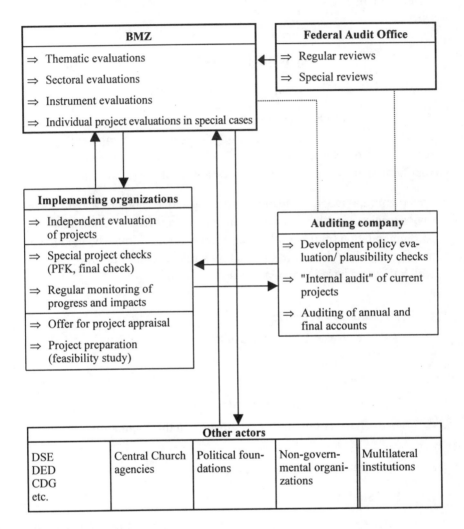

Source: Breier (1998b)

FEDERAL MINISTRY FOR ECONOMIC COOPERATION AND DEVELOPMENT

- Department 310 -   Bonn, January 1997

The BMZ's evaluation matrix

Terms of Reference (TOR)

The main report to be submitted by the evaluators must comply with the following pattern as closely as possibly for reasons of comparability. The pattern is also to be seen as a check list for the evaluation, which may be supplemented by lists of specific questions as the need arises.

Statements and recommendations presuppose one another. Statements on major weaknesses should be accompanied by a reference to the resulting recommendation (number of the recommendation). Similarly, the recommendations should be accompanied by a reference to the statements on which they are based (page, paragraph or point).

1   Preliminary remarks

—   cause and objective of the study

—   study methodology

—   study period

—   composition of the evaluation group

—   partner country's participation in the evaluation

2   Summary

2.1   Essential statements (points 3 to 9)

2.2   Essential recommendations (reference to person to whom recommendations are addressed)

3   General conditions (only if relevant to the project to be evaluated)

3.1   Political, economic, societal and socio-cultural factors in the partner country and the region (human rights situation, degree of legal certainty, rights of the people to participate [gender-differentiated], economic and social order, orientation of government action to development)

3.2   Brief analysis of the sector in which the project to be evaluated is located (overview of the main features of the sector, general economic conditions, sponsor structures, development prospects)

— private enterprises in the project environment providing relevant goods or services

— other bilateral projects of relevance to the private sector at government, meso and enterprise level

— distinction from or overlapping with corresponding private-sector promotional measures of other donors or initiatives taken by the developing country itself

3.3   Analysis

— of the counterpart organization (including the management's and staff's willingness and ability to perform)

— of limiting general conditions

— of informal organizational structures (prospects of decentralization, opportunities for networking governmental/non-governmental organizations, willingness to delegate, opportunities for developing alternative structures

— of opportunities for using domestic experts (rather than foreign experts)

4   Brief description of the project in tabular form

Implementing organization:

Project title:

Project number:

Project period:

Target group:

Overall goal:

Purpose of project:

Results sought:

Financial resources:

Manpower assignment (in expert-months):

— Long-term experts

— Short-term experts

Counterpart training:

Equipment deployed:

Counterpart organization in developing country:

Administrative basis:

Previous studies:

5.1   Partner country's objectives

5.2   Objectives of donor country (and of co-financier, if any)

5.3   Overall goal, purpose of project, project results specifically sought with relevant indicators, assumptions, comparative synoptic description based on project agreements and implementation offers and proposals, negotiating mandates

5.4   Analysis and evaluation of the objectives as regards:

— their compatibility as between donor and partner country

— their clarity and hierarchical breakdown

— their realism (is realistic account taken of the partner's options [general conditions]?)

— any adjustment/change made during the project

— account taken of coherence with objectives of other policies

— target groups identified (with distinction made between women and men)

— acceptance by the target group, its level of development (willingness and ability)

— direct/indirect structural poverty orientation

— staff training by partner

— account taken of women's interests

— account taken of environmental interests (if relevant)

— account taken of sustained significance

5.5 Overall evaluation of the purposes of project (was adequate account taken of general conditions relevant to the project and counterpart when the objectives were defined?)

6   Analysis and evaluation of planning

6.1 Does an analysis of needs (including an analysis by the counterpart) exist?

6.2 Compliance with the prescriptions of the country concept

6.3 Participation of the target group (with distinction made between women and men, which method of participation?) and counterpart

6.4 Coordination with other local agencies and other donors

6.5 Specialized and technical planning (location; choice of technology; environmental aspects; account taken of resources/institutions/experts available in partner country; M&E system)

6.6 Time sequence of planning (orientation phase, after-care phase)

6.7 Manpower assignment planning

6.8 Planning of local staff training (time, substance, instruments)

6.9 Cost estimate and financial planning

6.10 Assumptions and requirements

6.11   Adjustment of planning in subsequent course of project

6.12   Overall evaluation of planning (are the planned operations adequate and likely to achieve the objectives? Was account taken of aspects of sustained significance?)

7   Analysis and evaluation of implementation

7.1   Technical implementation, environment

7.2   Factor endowment (staff assigned, counterparts, physical resources, spare parts, funds, land law)

7.3   Organizational and institutional implementation (sponsor, participation of target group - with distinction made between women and men [which method of participation?] - use or integration of resources/institutions/experts available in partner country, donor coordination)

7.4   Local staff training (time, substance, instruments)

7.5   Departures from planning, satisfaction of requirements

7.6   General evaluation of implementation (including operating phase in case of financial cooperation) (was the vision underlying objectives/planning pursued in a workmanlike manner?)

8   Analysis and evaluation of project control

8.1   Levels of control
   — Partner country (decision-making bodies, project sponsor, counterpart, target group)
   — Implementing organization (GTZ, KfW, others)
   — Subcontractors (including consultancies, suppliers)
   — BMZ

8.2   Control instruments
   — Monitoring of operations, monitoring of impacts

- — Reporting
- — Progress reviews, evaluations
- — Project visits
- — Policy dialogue

8.3 Final evaluation

9 Effectiveness in development terms

9.1 Project results and achievement of the purposes of the project (causes of any departures from planning)

9.2 Evaluation of cost-benefit ratio

9.3 Economic, social, ecological and socio-cultural impacts (with distinction made between women and men, where possible)

9.3.1 Impacts on

- — incomes
- — employment
- — balance of payments
- — partner country's budget
- — regional and sectoral linkages
- — sponsor institutions (decentralization, delegation, networking, development of alternative structures)
- — sponsor institution's budget
- — training of sponsor institution's staff
- — situation of the poor (participation, promotion of productive forces)
- — mobilization of self-help
- — situation of women (e.g. workload, income, education/ training, health, nutrition, social and legal position)

9.3.2 Consequences of use of technologies transferred

- — technological competence

—   assessment of consequences of technology

9.3.3   Ecological impacts
—   actual or likely positive or negative environmental impacts
—   risks after project is completed

9.3.4   Socio-cultural impacts
—   legitimacy/acceptance by the target group (gender-differentiated to ensure necessary motivation for sustained functioning)
—   effects on the target group's cultural identity

9.4   Sustained significance of the project

9.5   Overall evaluation of effectiveness on development terms

10   Recommendations (based on knowledge acquired from evaluated project)

10.1   Recommendations concerning specific project - addressed to whom? - (corresponds to Statement No ..., page ...)

10.2   Recommendations concerning specific sector - addressed to whom? - (corresponds to Statement No ..., page ...)

10.3   Macrospecific recommendations - addressed to whom? - (corresponds to Statement No ..., page ...)

11   General conclusions (lessons learned, derived from knowledge acquired from evaluated project)

11.1   for project type (including its suitability to act as a model)

11.2   for the subsector or sector as a whole

11.3   as regards methods and tools

12   Other findings (based on consultants' empirical knowledge)

13 Annex

13.1 Travel and work flow

13.2 Sources (interlocutors, documents, specialized literature, primary surveys, etc.)

13.3 General map

13.4 Overviews in the form of tables

13.5 Preliminary report

Annex 2

Table A1:   Trend analysis for Ouassala

Criteria	1988	'89	'90	'91	'92	'93	'94	'95	'96	'97	Trend '92-'97
					← PGRN begins						
Improvement or impoverishment of livelihoods											
Agricultural yields	•••	••••	•••••	•••••	••	•••••	••••	•••	•••	•••	+/-
Family incomes	•	•	•	•	••	•••	•••	•••	•••	•••	++
Consumer prices of grain	••	•••	••••	•••	••	•••••	••••	••	•••	•••	-
Health status of children	••	•••	•••	•••	•••	••	•	••	•	•	--
Access or exclusion from resources											
Access to firewood	•••	•••	•••	••	••	••	•	•	•	•	-
Access to drinking water	••	••	•••••	•••	••••	•••	•••	•••	•••	•••	+/-
Access to the market	••	••	••	•••	•••	•••	•••	••••	••••	••••	+/-
Access to means of transport	••	••	•••	••	••	•••	••	••••	••••	••••	++
Access to fertile land	••	••	••	••	••	•••	•••	••••	••••	••••	++
Expansion or reduction of knowledge											
School enrolment rate	••	••	••	•••	•••	••••	••••	•••••	•••••	••••	++
Knowledge of sustainable land use	••	••	••	••	••••	••••	••••	•••	•••	••	+/-
Participation in or alienation from rights											
Conflicts between farmers and herderms[a]	••••	••••	••••	••••	••••	••••	••••	••••	••	•••	-
Migration[b]	••	••	••	••	•••	••••	••••	••••	••••	••••	+

Remarks:
a   The higher the number of points, the smaller the number of conflicts.
b   The higher the number of points, the less migration there is.

Key:
••••• = very good
•••• = good
••• = fair
•• = poor
• = very poor

Table A2: Trend analysis for Damba

Criteria	Year 1980	'81	'82	'83	'84	'85	'86	'87	'88	'89	'90	'91	'92	'93	'94	'95	'96	'97	Trend '94–97
Improvement or impoverishment of livelihoods																			
Agricultural yields	•••	••	••	•	•	•••	••••	••••	•••	••••	••••	••••	••••	••••	••••	••••	•••••	•••[a]	+/–
Family incomes	••	••	••	•	•	•••	••••	•••	•••	•••	•••	••••	••••	•••••	••••	••••	••••	•••[a]	+/–
Consumer prices of grain	••	••			•	•••	••••	•••	•••	•••	•••	•••	•••	•••••	•••	•••	•••	•••	–
Health status of children	••	••	••	•	••	••	•••	•	•••		•••	••	••	•	••	••	•	••	+
Access or exclusion from resources																			
Access to firewood	••••	••••	••••	•••	•••	•••	•••	•••	•••	•••	•••	•••	•••	•••	•••	•••	•••	•••	+
Access to drinking water	•	•	•			••	•	•	•••	•••	•••	•••	•••	•••	•••	•••	•••	•••	+/–
Access to the market	••	••	••	••	••	••	••	••	••	•••	••	•••	•••	•••	•••	•••	•••	•••	+ +
Access to means of transport	••	••	••	••	••	••	••	••	••	••	••	••	••	••	••	••	••	•••	+ +
Access to fertile land	•	•	•	•	•	•	••	•	•	•	•	•	•	•	•	•	•	••	+
Expansion or reduction of knowledge																			
School enrolment rate	••	•	••	••	••	••	••	•••	•••	••••	••••	••••	•••	••••	•••	••••	••••	••••	+/–
Knowledge of sustainable land use	•	•	••	••	••	••	•••	•••	•••	•••	•••	•••	•••	•••	•••	•••	•••	•••	+
Participation in or alienation from rights																			
Conflicts between farmers and herders[b]	••••	••	••••	••••	••••	••••	••••	••••	••••	••••	••••	••••	•••	••	••	••	••	•	+/–
Migration[c]	••	••	••	••	••	••	••	••	••	••	••	••	••	••••	••••	••••	••••	•••••	+

Key:
•••• = very good
••• = good
•• = fair
• = bad
. = very bad

Remarks:
a Incomes fell in 1997 because of several collections to finance village projects.
b The higher the number of points, the lower the number of conflicts.
c The higher the number of points, the less migration there is.

PGRN begins →

Table A3:   Activity list for Ouassala

Activity	Organization	Importance for daily life	Beneficiary group Women (W) / Men (M)	Labour expended Installation	Labour expended Mainte- nance
Health station	World Bank, et al.	●●●●●	M + W	●●●●●	●
Grain bank	PGRN	●●●●●	M + W	●●●	●●●
Vegetable growing	PGRN	●●●●●	M + W	●●●●●	●●●●
School/furnishing	PGRN	●●●●●	M + W	●●●●	●●
Functional literacy	PIDEB and others	●●●●	M + W	●●	●
Provision of donkey carts	PGRN	●●●●	M	●●●	●●
Stone lines	PGRN	●●●●	M	●●●●●	●●
Composting facilities / organic manuring	PGRN	●●●	M	●●●●●	●●●●●●
Pump for the well	CLD	●●●	M + W	●●	●●
Tree nursery	PGRN	●●●	M	●●	●●
Hedges	PGRN	●●	M + W	●●●	●●
Sheep fattening	PGRN	●●	W	●●	●●●
Millet mills	(?)	●	W	●●	●●
Nature reserves	PGRN	●	M	●●	●●
Tree planting	PGRN/PIDEB	●	M	●●	●●
Bee-keeping	PGRN	●	M	●●●	●●●

Key:
●●●●● = very important / very considerable effort
●●●●   = important / considerable effort
●●●   = fairly important / medium amount of effort
●●   = of minor importance / little effort
●   = no importance / no effort

Table A4: Activity list for Damba

Activity	Organization	Importance/benefit	Proportion of population[a]	Beneficiary group[b] Men (M)/women (W)	Labour expended Installation Men / women	Labour expended Maintenance Men / women	Financial expenditure Installation	Financial expenditure Maintenance
Grain bank	PGRN	●●●●●●[c]	●●●●●	M + W	●●●●● M + W	●● M	●	●●
Stone lines	PGRN	●●●●●	●●●	M	●●●●● M	●● M	●	●
Donkey carts	PGRN	●●●●●	●●●	M	● M	●● M	●●●	●●●●
Mosque roof	Migrants	●●●●●	●●●●●	M + W	●●●●● M + W	●●● M + W	●●●	●●●●
Agricultural equipment	PIDEP	●●●●	●●●●	M	● M	● M	●	●●●●
Tree plantations	PGRN	●●●●	●●●●	M	●●●●● M	●●●●● M	●	●
Literacy	PIDEP / PGRN	●●●●	●●●●	M + W	●●● M + W	●● M	●	●●●
Improved stoves	Eau et Forêt	●●●●	●●●●●	M	●●● M	●● M	●	●
Improved chicken breeding[d]	PIDEP	●●●	●●	M	●●● M	●●● M	●	●
Vegetable growing	PIDEP	●●●	●●●●●	M	●●●● M	●●● M	●●	●●●
Well pump	IJA	●●●	●●●●●	M + W	●● M + W	●● M + W	●	●●●●
Groundnut presses	(?)	●●●	●●	W	●●●●● M	●●● W	●	●●
Tree nursery	PGRN	●●●	●●	M	●●●●● M	●●●● W	●	●
Composting facilities / organic manuring	PGRN	●●[e]	●●●	M	●●● M	●● M	●	●
Sheep fattening	IJA	●	●●	M + W	●●● M + W	●●● M + W	●	●●

Remarks:

a   This column as completed after a wide range of observations by the team.

b   The farmers always benefit; the herders can benefit only from the communal projects (health station, well).

c   The participants introduced a six-point scale to single out what they saw as the incomparable benefits of the grain bank.

d   A more productive breed of breeding cocks was introduced for hybridization purposes. The hybrids have survived so far. The building of special chicken coops, which had been supported by PIDEB, was abandoned by the villagers because it entailed too much labour.

The recommendation that the chickens be given termites to eat was accepted.

e   No benefit yet because the activity has only just begun.

Key:

●●●●●● = extremely important / extreme effort (the target groups insisted on being able to award 6 points)

●●●●● = very important / a great deal of effort

●●●● = important / considerable effort

●●● = fairly important / medium effort

●● = hardly important / little effort

● = unimportant / no effort

Table A5:   Influence matrix for Ouassala

Criteria	Organic manuring	Stone walls	Nature reserve	Irrigated vegetable growing	Donkey carts	Well pump	Sheep fattening	Health station	Tree nursery	Bee-keeping	Hedges	Grain mills	Literacy	Grain bank	Tree planting	School	Σ passive +152/-7
Improvement or impoverishment of livelihoods																	
Agricultural yields	4	4	1	3	4	0[a]	3	0	0	0	2	0	2	0	1	0[b]	+24
Family incomes	3	3	2	3	4	-1	4	0	2	0	0	0	0	3	0	-1	+24 / -2
Health status of children	0	0	0	2	4[c]	4	0	4	0	0	0	0	0	1	0	0	+15
Access to or exclusion from resources																	
firewood	0	0	0	0	2	0	0	0	0	0	0	0	0	0	0[d]	0	+2
drinking water	0	0	0	0	0	4	0	0	0	0	0	0	3	0	0	0	+7
the market	1	0	0	0	4	0	0	0	0	0	0	0	0	1	0	0	+6
means of transport	0	0	0	0	4	0	2	0	0	0	0	0	0	0	0	0	+4
fertile land	4	4	4	2	4	3	2	0	3	0	0	0	2	1	0	0	+27
Expansion or reduction of knowledge																	
of sustainable land use	4	4	4	2	4	0	3	0	3	0	1	0	2	2	1	0	+27
School enrolment rate	0	0	0	0	0	0	0	0	0	0	0	0	0	0	0	4	+4
Participation or alienation from rights																	
Land use conflicts	0	0	-4	0	0	3[e]	0	1	0	0	0	0	0	1	-1	0	+5 / -5
Migration	0	0	0	2	2	0	0	0	0	0	0	0	0	1	0	2	+8
Σ active +159/-7	+16	+15	+11/-4	+14	+32	+14/-1	+12	+5	+8	0[f]	+3	0[g]	+9	+10	+2[h]/-1	+6/-1	

Key: 0 = no influence; 1 = little influence; 2 = medium influence; 3 = strong influence; 4 = very strong influence; A '-' before a figure means a negative influence

Remarks:
The question always asked during the discussion was: How does project activity x, as it currently exists or functions in your village, influence social criterion y?.
a) The cost of repairing the pump is high and reduces our income. b) School fees are a burden on income. c) For one thing, sick children can be transported; for another, you can go to market and buy medicines for the children. d) The trees are not big enough yet to produce any firewood. e) As a result of the common well we come together more and understand each other better. f) The few families affected by this have obviously been unable to derive any benefit from the operations. g) The mill stood idle because the women could not raise any money for the diesel fuel. h) The trees are still too small for any benefit to be derived from them.

Table A6: Influence matrix for Damba

Criteria	Agricultural equipment	Improved poultry breeding	Irrigated vegetable growing	Well pump	Tree plantations	Literacy	Donkey carts	Improved stoves	Grain bank	Stone lines	Organic manuring	Mosque roof	Health station	Tree Nursery	School (Ouassala)	Σ passive +97/–4
Improvement or impoverishment of livelihoods																
Agricultural yields	3	0	0b	0	0	0	3	0	2	3	0	0	2	0	0	+13
Family incomes	3	2	2	0	0	2	2	0	2	2	0	0	2	0	0	+17
Health status of children	2	2	0	2	0	2	0	0	2	0	0	0	3	0	2c	+15
Access to or exclusion from resources																
firewood	0	0	0	0	0	0	3	1	0	0	0	0	0	0	0	+4
drinking water	0	0	0	4	0	0	0	0	0	0	0	0	0	0	0	+4
the market	0	0	0	0	0	0	3	0	3	0	0	0	0	0	0	+6
means of transport	0	0	0	0	0	0	3	0	0	0	0	0	0	0	0	+5
fertile land	0d –2	0	0	0	0	0	3	0	0	0	0	0	0	0	0	–2
Expansion or reduction of knowledge																
of sustainable land use	1	0	1	2	3	3	3e	2	2	3	0	0	0	2	1	+23
School enrolment rate	0	0	0	0	0	1	0	0	2	0	0	0	0	0	4	+5
Participation or alienation from rights																
Land use conflicts	0	0	0	0	0	0	0	0	0	–2f	0	2	2g	0	0	–4 –2
Σ active +96/–3	+9 –1	+4	+3	+8	+3	+8	+20	+3	+11	+8 –2	0	+2	+9	+2	+5	

Remarks:

a No influence yet because the operation has only just begun.
b A bad site was chosen for gardening, and yields have been low.
c The school in Ouassala is also attended by Damba's children. There is a vaccination service at the school.
d Extensive ploughing has made the land even less fertile.
e Indirect influence due to the saving of time, which benefits joint land use planning. The target groups insisted on this evaluation, even though they had really only been asked about direct influences.
f The stone lines have blocked some paths and are removed and not replaced by passing people and herds.
g Conflicts between population groups have been reduced by the joint building and use of the health centre.

Key:

0 = no influence
1 = little influence
2 = medium influence
3 = strong influence
4 = very strong influence
A '-' before a figure means a negative influence.

Figure A1:   Life line of Ouassala village

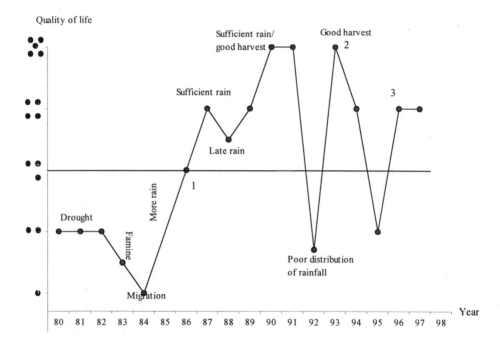

1:   The harvest was only moderate because the rain caused erosion.

2:   Adequate harvest plus external aid because of the failed harvest of 1992.

3:   There were also families who had a very good harvest that year.

Key:

Figure A2:   Life line of Damba village

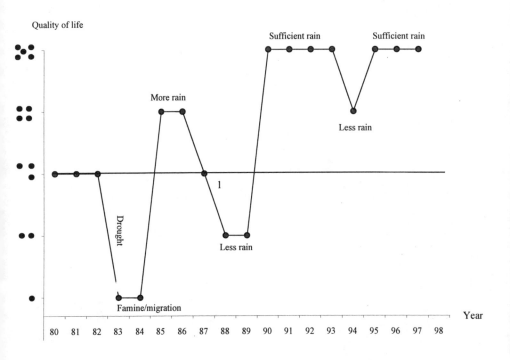

1:    Sufficient rainfall, but a bushfire threatened our village. We had to pay a fine, and some of our
     harvest was burnt.

Key:

= very good   = good   = fair   ● ● = poor   ● = very poor